MASTERING THE MICRO

USING THE MICROCOMPUTER IN THE ELEMENTARY CLASSROOM

DOROTHY H. JUDD
ROBERT C. JUDD

Scott, Foresman and Company
Glenview, Illinois

Dallas, Texas • Oakland, New Jersey • Palo Alto, California • Tucker, Georgia • London

No part of this book may be reproduced in any form or by any means, except those portions intended for classroom use, without permission in writing from the publisher.

Library of Congress Cataloging in Publication Data

Judd, Dorothy H.
  Mastering the micro.

  Bibliography: p.
  Includes index.
  1. Computer-assisted instruction—United States.
2. Computer-assisted instruction—Computer programs.
3. Education, Elementary—United States—Data processing.
I. Judd, Robert C. II. Title.
LB1028.5.J83 1984   372.13'9445   83-20380
ISBN 0-673-15909-4

Copyright © 1984 Scott, Foresman and Company.

All rights reserved.

Printed in the United States of America.

1 2 3 4 5 6 MAL 88 87 86 85 84 83

PREFACE

"How can I use the microcomputer to increase the effectiveness of teaching and learning for children?" is a question that is often asked. This book answers that question by discussing ways the microcomputer is used to provide instructional reinforcement in the classroom. This book provides both preservice and inservice teachers with useful information about microcomputers and their classroom uses. Each chapter focuses on teaching strategies and techniques at the elementary level, but the secondary teacher of a subject other than computer programming or mathematics will also find ideas that are useful. We believe that teachers will find that many of the microcomputer-related learning experiences discussed in this book can be integrated into their curriculums.

The activities described at the end of each chapter will be a valuable resource for teachers who are seeking ways to integrate a microcomputer into the teaching and learning styles of their classrooms. Teachers are encouraged to complete each activity because our experience shows that in this way teachers gain valuable insight about student use. Completing the activities also helps teachers create useful visual aids and display material for their classrooms. Not every activity will fit the teaching and learning style of every teacher. We want to encourage teachers to adapt the ideas presented in this book to the needs that each one faces.

Chapter one discusses the uses of microcomputer instruction and its importance in classrooms across the country. Teachers at all grade levels, in every discipline, and with all types of students will find ideas in this book on how they can use microcomputers to enhance the quality of student learning, regardless of whether one or many microcomputers are available in a classroom. Scenarios involving the use of microcomputers in elementary classrooms provide a description of computer assisted instruction (CAI) that is especially useful. There are eight activities at the end of Chapter one. Two of these involve identifying issues and current developments in the information age. The other six activities call for hands-on experience with the microcomputer keyboard and running prepared programs.

Chapter two describes the variety of software available and the evaluation guidelines that can aid a teacher in making satisfactory choices. It also explains the value of drill and practice that use microcomputer programs, as well as the cost effectiveness of using microcomputers for science and social studies simulations. Educational questions about graphics, sound, and color capabilities of microcomputers are considered. Ways that LOGO, PILOT, and BASIC provide students with a means of control over the microcomputer are given. The activities at the end of Chapter two build on the experience gained from using Chapter one activities. Both teachers and students will benefit from using the LOGO Discovery activity and running the suggested CAI programs. One of the activities in Chapter two calls for discovering the steps required in solving a problem that forms the logic needed for a programming challenge in a Chapter three activity.

Chapter three provides an overview of the choices facing teachers who want to create tailor-made programs for their students. We not only describe the usefulness of the PILOT language and authoring systems, but also describe and illustrate teacher aids for developing CAI. In addition, the chapter outlines ways students and teachers can create printed material using word-processing programs. The nine activities at the end of Chapter three provide PILOT, BASIC, and word-processing opportunities.

Chapter four considers the research evidence on the effectiveness of CAI at the elementary, junior high, and high school level. We provide a description of the benefits of microcomputer use for teachers, students, and administrators. Teachers who are new to the use of microcomputers will find the "Microcomputer Use in Second Grade" or the "Microcomputer Use in Fifth Grade" sections especially helpful. The five activities at the end of Chapter four give the teacher an opportunity to modify a program, to convert a storyboard to a CAI program, to evaluate a microcomputer program, to create a quiz or worksheet using a word-processing program, and to use an item analysis program to discover the reteaching needed.

Chapter five describes teacher utility programs that make the record-keeping burden of the teacher easier. The challenge for teachers is to include microcomputer use in their classroom planning and to integrate such use into their curriculums. Many teachers will find the "What Can You Begin Doing?" section especially helpful. The sequence of learning is completed with additional information in the Appendix that includes the Glossary, Recommended Readings and Media, and the Materials Resource List.

The contents of each chapter were tested in the classroom in teacher inservice sessions and in preservice teacher curriculum courses. Some of the activities are now part of a set of Study-Pacs integrated into three required professional semesters in elementary education at Northern Illinois University.

This book began with classroom experiences of pioneering teachers in Hinsdale, a suburb of Chicago. In the summer of 1980, these teachers took time from vacations to complete a course in microcomputer instructional applications taught jointly by the authors of this book. To those teachers and the many teachers and teacher candidates in the classes and workshops given by the authors since that time, this book owes it existence and is gratefully dedicated.

Serendipity deserves second billing in these acknowledgments. This text could not have taken shape had not one of the authors brought home a microcomputer, unannounced and without consultation, in the summer of 1978. What followed was a classic case of "if you can't beat them, join them." Dr. Margaret Carroll, Professor Emeritus of Northern Illinois

University, and Dr. Raymond B. Fox were important motivating forces in the writing of this book.

The others who helped shape the content of these pages are too numerous to list. The suggestions and favorable reactions of many teachers and faculty colleagues who were part of audiences in more than forty presentations on microcomputer instructional use by one or both of the authors is gratefully acknowledged. No book can take its final form without the care and tending of an editor and the reviewers. Chris Jennison was a superb editor with whom to work. The reviewers who contributed much to the final form of this book were Dan Dolan of the Montana Office of Public Instruction, Helena, Montana, Richard H. King, Coordinator of Computer Sciences, Essex Junction, Vermont, and Professor Rich Hamblin of California State Polytechnic University, Pomona, California. Our thanks to each of them, but special thanks go to Dan Dolan for work that represented significant insight and labor above and beyond the duty of a reviewer.

CONTENTS

1 Microcomputer Instruction   1
   Microcomputers and Society   2
   CAI Utilization by Subject Areas, Grade Levels, and
     Student Types   4
   Types of Programs   8
   Location and Scheduling Factors   10
   Creating a Teaching and Learning Climate   11
   ACTIVITY ONE—MICROCOMPUTERS AND SOCIETY   19
   ACTIVITY TWO—MICROCOMPUTER FAMILIARIZATION I   20
   ACTIVITY THREE—INFORMATION AGE   22
   ACTIVITY FOUR—MICROCOMPUTER FAMILIARIZATION
     II   23
   ACTIVITY FIVE—MICROCOMPUTER FAMILIARIZATION
     III   25
   ACTIVITY SIX—MICROCOMPUTER FAMILIARIZATION IV   26
   ACTIVITY SEVEN—MICROCOMPUTER FAMILIARIZATION
     V   27
   ACTIVITY EIGHT—MICROCOMPUTER FAMILIARIZATION
     VI   28

2 Microcomputer Software   33
   Teaching and Learning Microcomputer Programs   33
   Why Use Drill Courseware?   34
   Why Use Problem-Solving Courseware?   36
   Why Use Tutorial Courseware?   37
   Why Use Simulation Courseware?   38
   Ways to Use Logo, Pilot, and Basic Programming Resources   40
   Courseware or Program Sources   44
   Criteria for Software Selection   46
   Ease of Customizing Software   48
   Graphics, Sound, and Color Factors in Program Selection   49
   ACTIVITY ONE—LOGO DISCOVERY   52
   ACTIVITY TWO—SIMPLE PROGRAMMING IN BASIC   53
   ACTIVITY THREE—PROBLEM-SOLVING PROCESS   54
   ACTIVITY FOUR—RUNNING A CAI PROGRAM   55
   ACTIVITY FIVE—RUNNING A CAI DRILL AND PRACTICE
     PROGRAM   56
   ACTIVITY SIX—RUNNING A CAI SIMULATION PROGRAM   57

viii Contents

3 Teacher-Made Instructional Programs 61
Pilot as an Authoring Aid 63
Authoring Systems for CAI Programs 65
Word-Processing Programs for Student Reading and Writing 72
Word-Processing Programs for Teacher-Generated
  Print Materials 78
ACTIVITY ONE—SIMPLE PROGRAMMING IN PILOT 82
ACTIVITY TWO—ADDITIONAL PROGRAMMING IN PILOT 84
ACTIVITY THREE—WORD PROCESSING 84
ACTIVITY FOUR—CONVERTING PROBLEM-SOLVING
  PROCESS TO PROGRAMMING SOLUTION 85
ACTIVITY FIVE—ADDITIONAL WORD PROCESSING 86
ACTIVITY SIX—PROGRAMMING A WORD PROBLEM USING
  PILOT 87
ACTIVITY SEVEN—PROGRAMMING A WORD PROBLEM USING
  BASIC 88
ACTIVITY EIGHT—USING THE PILOT J COMMAND 89
ACTIVITY NINE—CONVERTING BETWEEN PILOT
  AND BASIC 90

4 Implications of CAI and CMI 93
What Does Research Suggest About Expectations? 93
What Benefits for the Teacher? 96
What Benefits for the Student? 104
What Benefits for the Administrator? 106
ACTIVITY ONE—MODIFYING A CAI PROGRAM 110
ACTIVITY TWO—CONVERTING A STORYBOARD TO
  A PROGRAM 111
ACTIVITY THREE—EVALUATING SOFTWARE
  PROGRAMS 112
ACTIVITY FOUR—CREATING A WORKSHEET OR QUIZ 113
ACTIVITY FIVE—USING "QUIZSTAT" 114

5 What Else Can a Microcomputer Do for
     Instruction? 117
How Can a Gradebook Program Help? 118
Readability Evaluations and Other Analytic Uses 120
Curriculum Design and Development: Challenge for Teachers 126
What Can You Begin Doing? 130

Appendix
Glossary 133
Recommended Readings and Media 138
Materials Resource List 144
Index 148

1
MICROCOMPUTER INSTRUCTION

The warning call of a traditional children's game goes, "Here I come, ready or not!" In the 1980s, this could be the warning call from microcomputers to teachers as these electronic learning tools move us all into the information age.

Students attending school today and tomorrow are and will be part of the information age. During their lives, these learners will experience the benefits and challenges of microcomputers in society. Teachers have at their fingertips an instructional tool about which too many know too little. The goal of this book is to ease the transition from the world of learning as teachers knew it in the past to the world of learning as today's and tomorrow's students will experience it. The most heartening aspect of the future is that including microcomputers in the instructional scene will encourage a change in the role of teachers from taskmaster to facilitator of learning.

Some of the tedious elements of teaching, such as grading drill and practice exercises, keeping records, averaging grades, and determining the instructional level at which students are ready to work, can be eased by the use of the microcomputer and software programs. The basic skills of reading, writing, and arithmetic will probably be required learning for many years to come. Much of the reinforcing of these basic skills can be assumed by the microcomputer. Even some part of the initial instruction of basic skills can be provided in a microcomputer mode. As the teacher is freed from routine time-consuming tasks, a more creative teaching role can emerge. The teacher can give more emphasis to the human aspects of education, such as helping students to

1. Fulfill personal needs and engage in learning at a higher level
2. Discuss human beings and their interactions
3. Discover meaningful and individualized learning programs
4. Develop social interaction and responsibility

Teaching styles and learning styles are both likely to change as a result of the use of microcomputers. These changes in learning patterns will provide better opportunities for developing problem-solving skills as well as decision-making skills. The opportunity to make choices in computer simulations and problem-solving activities will be welcomed.

The microcomputer is already making possible a more complete record-keeping function in the classrooms where teachers have access to a microcomputer and an appropriate record-keeping program. Many of the computer-assisted instruction (CAI) programs that are available create a record of student performance far more detailed than the typical teacher kept in a grade book before microcomputers were available. The best CAI programs indicate not only the completion of a lesson, but also list the errors and number of attempts made, the time used by the student in completing the lesson, and a summary of statistics that shows how a given student compares with peer performance. These readily available records can make possible better insight into the learning needs of the student and can help the teacher individualize and personalize the application of a curriculum. The microcomputer can provide needed assistance to the classroom teacher in creating a cost-effective learning environment that is individualized, humanistic, and oriented to basic skills and problem solving. These are worthwhile goals for the 1980s and beyond.

MICROCOMPUTERS AND SOCIETY

There is a new partner in the education process, the microcomputer and its programs. School administrators, curriculum supervisors, education agencies, and the teacher-training institutions throughout the country are also considering the implications of the advent of the microcomputer.

As it is with most innovations, society is concerned about the uses and abuses of microcomputers in schools. Knowledge of what microcomputers can and cannot do is needed for rational decisions by educational leaders. Moreover, society must consider the economic, social, and psychological impact of microcomputers on individuals, on subgroups within our society, and on the whole of society. These concerns will require teachers to consider such problems as

- What constitutes misuse of a computer?
- Where can microcomputers provide unique learning advantages?

Uses of the computer.

- How does one deal with the rapid pace of change in technology?
- Why, in a microcomputer world, is learning of subject matter like long division, logarithms, and similar subjects necessary?
- How can we provide students with equitable experiences using the microcomputer in a time of shrinking enrollments and budgets?

Many of the difficulties currently faced by society and by educational institutions have been blamed on blindly trusting technology to find answers to the problems technology has created. Teachers and educational leaders need to carefully consider the role of the microcomputer in education for the 1980s.

CAI UTILIZATION BY SUBJECT AREAS, GRADE LEVELS, AND STUDENT TYPES

CAI raises immediate questions among teachers about whether the microcomputer should be used as a teacher or as a tool for teaching. This is understandable because the microcomputer, as a teacher, is a patient drillmaster, an effective tutor, a careful and precise evaluator of student work, and an accurate record keeper of student performance. On the other hand, the computer as a learning tool is a method of implementing new strategies, a way students can become independent learners, and a laboratory in which students can explore several avenues of learning. One of the persistent myths about computers is that they are only useful in terms of mathematics and science. This science-and-mathematics stereotype may have had some justification in the days of time-sharing with large computers because there were almost no other kinds of programs available. The CONDUIT organization in Iowa pioneered providing significant learning experiences in science using large computers as the learning vehicle. The PLATO series by the Control Data Corporation provided learning materials in a broad range of subjects, but use of this learning resource was limited to affluent school districts. In almost every instance where CAI was available from the large computers, the teachers using this mode of instructional assistance tended to have mathematics and science backgrounds.

The advent of the microcomputer changed all of those earlier patterns of computer use. An interesting story about a Florida teacher of English who wanted to use the microcomputer in teaching her students is worth repeating. She was told it was not possible to use the microcomputer as a vehicle for instruction in her English classes, so she decided to learn as much as she could about microcomputers. To assist in her effort, she found a young student who was enthusiastically involved in programming, and together they created a series of learning experiences for her English students on the microcomputer. The early history of microcomputer use in schools is enriched by similar stories of teachers who did not accept the phrase, "It can't be done."

A useful source of microcomputer programs is the Minnesota Educational Computer Consortium (MECC). MECC has developed a number of types of programs that are outstanding in the development of simulations. Consider the following sampling of MECC simulation programs[1]:

"Civil War"—a simulation of 14 Civil War battles

"Fish"—a graphic demonstration of blood circulation in an animal with a two-chambered heart

"Furs"—a simulation of the North American fur trade of the 1770s

"Minerals"—a unique program that puts the student in the role of a scientist who has to identify an unknown mineral

"Nomad"—a trip to grandma's house in an imaginary city

"Odell Lake"—a program that simulates the food chain for fish

"Oregon"—a trip to Oregon by covered wagon

"Sell Apples"—students decide how much to charge for their apples in a practical lesson on pricing

"Sell Bicycles"—two students manage separate bicycle companies and learn about competition, production, advertising, and pricing

"Sell Plants"—students learn whether advertising makes the difference when they try to sell 1,000 tomato plants

"Voyageur"—students are transformed into early 18th century woodsmen in the forests of northern Minnesota

Today, the publisher of traditional educational materials has software available in a broad range of learning modules

Today, publishers of traditional educational materials have software available in a broad range of learning modules.

or programs for various brands of microcomputers. As an example of the breadth of these offerings, consider the following excerpts from publisher's catalogs published recently.

> An ancient society is forced to leave their ancestral home. Students are members of that culture in this simulation. Tough decisions face them. Students must make choices about migration, trade, aggression, and building a palace.[2]

> This set of nine programs has been tested for more than two years in classrooms. Designed for prereaders and beginning readers, these programs feature extensive graphics. Three programs drill students on letters and sounds. Students' memory skills are reinforced through another three programs. Reinforcement of counting and addition skills is the focus of the remaining three pro-

grams. The teacher can select the words or letters used in two programs.[3]

Brief lessons and motivating exercises provide excellent practice on a variety of verb skills including verb recognition, regular and irregular tenses, correct usage, and more. Vocabulary level is controlled to correspond to the student's reading level and the three level format offers an additional challenge as skills grow. A student management system allows all student errors to be posted to the teacher's file.[4]

Used to build rate and comprehension in silent reading. This training bridges student from isolated word recognition to fluent silent reading. Student reviews key words in context sentences. Key words can be flashed tachistoscopically to build stronger word impressions. Program provides stationary training, left-to-right reading training, as well as a comprehension check.[5]

Designed to help students translate word problems into appropriate equations for solution. The unique capabilities of the computer and a variety of examples provide opportunities for the guess and check process where the student is encouraged to look for patterns, make generalizations, and interactively formulate rules.[6]

Provides instruction and highly motivating exercises in writing skills for students in fourth through eighth grades. Based on the strategy of sentence combining, by utilizing interesting graphical examples and practice exercises, students become familiar with various sentence structures and transfer them to their independent writings.[7]

Teachers can check the progress of children in certain individualized programs. Information about students, instructional objectives, and specific test items can be correlated and summarized for the publisher's mathematics program.[8]

By playing this game, children learn the eight directions of north, south, east, west, northeast, southeast, southwest, and northwest. They also learn to estimate the distance between two objects.[9]

Students are taught four problem-solving strategies: (1) looking for vocabulary clues for basic operations; (2) using systematic trial and error using implicit and explicit givens; (3) identifying alternative actions in multiple step problems by first identifying the overall goal, then selecting the subgoals required to reach the final goal.[10]

The preceding paragraphs describe software programs for use in a wide variety of subject areas. You may have noted that many of the programs had a graded structure spanning a number of elementary grades. Of course, instructional programs are available for use in secondary school and college. What may not have been as clearly evident is the availability of programs especially suitable for the learning-disabled as well as the gifted student. The Materials Resource list in the Appendix includes program sources for your consideration.

TYPES OF PROGRAMS

The frequency of student use depends not only on the number of microcomputers available, but also on the strategies you plan to employ when using microcomputers in a classroom or other learning site. Consider for a moment the alternative strategies a microcomputer makes possible in your students learning. At the very least you will want to plan for tutorials, drill, practice, testing, problem solving, and simulation. Each of these uses of the microcomputer can facilitate learning in almost every subject, at every grade level, and with every type of student.

Tutorials present information and then ask questions on the material presented. Because students can proceed at their own pace, these can be a valuable addition to the classroom regimen, especially with students who need more reinforcement of new content than their peers. Drill and practice programs also provide needed reinforcement for a broad spectrum of student abilities. Even gifted students occasionally may benefit from demonstrating their ability to themselves through a drill-and-practice opportunity on a microcomputer. Although some teachers will view a tutorial program as competition for their role as information giver, a good microcomputer tutorial can provide not only a controlled flow of information, but also helps the teacher by providing analysis of the answers given and keeping a record of the parts of the lesson to which a student responds especially well or poorly. The benefits of having each student answer every question, rather than sharing the answer with classmates, are impressive. Many teachers will not miss their earlier role in providing drill and practice learning opportunities for their students. The microcomputer provides a unique service in drill-and-practice sessions for students by keeping track of both right and wrong answers given, as well as the time a student takes to respond. The microcomputer is adaptable to either of the common strategies in presenting items for student response. The microcomputer can continue to present the same question until it has been answered correctly, then remove that question from the pool of questions being asked, or the microcomputer can proceed to ask a number of questions, returning to ask those questions again where a wrong answer was given. Because the microcomputer can painlessly keep track of almost any kind of detail, there is a thoroughness to microcomputer drill-and-practice lesson presentation that few teachers could duplicate.

Although limited microcomputer availability has led many teachers to use the microcomputer solely for drill and practice, one should not overlook considering the abilities of the microcomputer in providing problem-solving and simulation-learning opportunities. In problem solving, the microcomputer can painstakingly guide students in the problem solving process, enforcing correct approaches. As any teacher of arithmetic can attest, checking for a correct process is more demanding than checking for a correct answer. The microcomputer does not have difficulty following problem-solving processes because it is tuned in to each step along the way to the answer. On the other hand, the teacher must work back from the answer through the often scribbled maze of steps leading to an answer. Similarly, the microcomputer can create a simulated environment for a student, as in a science experiment too dangerous to actually perform. As an example, in a science class, the mixture of the wrong ingredients could cause an explosion. The teacher cannot tolerate the possibility of a real explosion in the classroom or lab, whereas the microcomputer can painlessly let the student learn from mistakes.

LOCATION AND SCHEDULING FACTORS

You may have heard stories of schools where a teacher finds a microcomputer gathering dust in a closet because the microcomputer was sent to the school without anyone knowing of its arrival. There are also reports of language arts teachers discovering that the mathematics or science teacher has a microcomputer and on inquiring of the principal, the teacher is told that the principal was not aware that anyone except math or science teachers would be interested. You may encounter a variety of such situations that will affect the location and scheduling of microcomputers in your school. There are as many possibilities for microcomputer location as there are arrangements of classrooms and learning resource centers. Teachers should be consulted about where the microcomputers are to be located. If there are enough machines so that every classroom is to have its share, you then will be faced with deciding where in your classroom you want them. A more common problem will be whether you want the microcomputers to be located in a central place where you can bring your students to work on them, or whether you and your fellow teachers want the microcomputers shifted from room to room according to a schedule.

Because you will be most concerned with location factors in your own classroom, it may help to realize that the principles governing the location of reading and other student-activity centers are reported to be applicable in the location of microcomputer-study areas. This is likely to mean that you need to plan on two student-size chairs for each microcomputer, with the possibility of pulling up two or three more chairs. Many of the simulations and even some of the problem-solving programs encourage team involvement, allowing three to five students to participate effectively. A corner of your room may be a better location than any other choice, although availability of power outlets and freedom from strong sunlight and its glare on the screen (or monitor) may also influence your choice. A later chapter provides some ideas on using and scheduling microcomputers among several grades. The best that is presently known suggests that 10 to 15 minutes of microcomputer activity for a student in elementary school is well within their attention span. Even a single microcomputer in a class of 30 students can have considerable impact if it is available for use throughout the year, even if only as often as one day per week. The teacher's role in the context of planning for microcomputer activity is not that different from the teacher's role in planning for reading or other group learning activities so common in the elementary grades.

CREATING A TEACHING AND LEARNING CLIMATE

In the pages that follow, you will find reports of actual microcomputer use in classrooms, learning resource centers, and microcomputer labs throughout the country. Wherever possible, the physical setting and the brand of microcomputer used, as well as the microcomputer activity involved, will be given. The common thread throughout is the success reported in creating a teaching and learning climate involving student use of microcomputers and the programs that run in them.

SETTING: The second grade has 17 students in a Texas rural school and is divided into four groups. One group of four children is gathered around the microcomputers.

MICROCOMPUTER: Two TI-99/4A microcomputers with speech synthesizers and video monitors are mounted on a low desk. The two microcomputers are separated from each other by a cardboard divider.

ACTIVITY: The students work in pairs in reading a story in their "Reading Is Fun" program.[11] This is a story planned to present them with a problem to solve. The two children are using headsets and will each simultaneously hear the story over their headsets and then respond to questions posed for them by the microcomputer in a "try it

12   *Microcomputer Instruction*

Creating a teaching/learning climate.

out" mode. One group has finished using the microcomputers and is busy with a paper-and-pencil exercise that is related to the story they have just read. The first group had 15 minutes on the machines, and each of the other groups will have about the same amount of time. The teacher is monitoring the use of the microcomputers while working with students in the group that is waiting their turn on the machines. When the students in the first group finish their paper-and-pencil activity, they will be ready to read the "The Carnival From Outer Space" story (in a book), the problem and vocabulary of which parallel the microcomputer story experience they have had.

SETTING: Twenty-seven students in a seventh grade mathematics class in a suburban school are with their teacher and the microcomputer coordinator for the school.
MICROCOMPUTER: A TRS-80, Model I, with a large

television screen attached, is mounted on a rolling cart at the front of the classroom.

ACTIVITY: Students are experiencing their first lesson on creating a microcomputer program to solve last week's math problems using the PILOT language for the task. The math teacher is at the keyboard of the TRS-80 while the microcomputer coordinator explains the program lines that the math teacher is typing on the computer keyboard. The students can see not only the PILOT commands but also the result of the commands or the solution to the problem appear on the screen instantaneously. After the 20-minute demonstration, students are expected to begin their programming effort. Thus, the students are directed to use the one-page handout on PILOT language to create with pencil and paper a four line program to solve any part of one problem from their math assignment. On this first day of microcomputer exposure, the math teacher is at the keyboard typing. Three of the students finish their pencil-and paper program before the bell rings and the teacher types their four-line programs on the computer keyboard, one at a time, and saves each program on disk, using the student's name as a file name. Two of the three programs run without further student work, bringing considerable pleasure to the boy and the girl who wrote the programs. Another student is crestfallen because her program will not run. As the bell rings, students are told to finish their pencil-and-paper programs because they will have another chance to run their work the next day.

SETTING: A second grade class of 23 students and their teacher in a small urban school are gathered around a microcomputer in one corner of the room.

MICROCOMPUTER: An Apple II with a black-and-white monitor is placed on a low school table. Beside the microcomputer is an Apple Silentype Printer.

ACTIVITY: The teacher is explaining that she will be using the microcomputer today, instead of the flipchart, to record the students' ideas for a story. The "Bank Street Writer"[12] word-processing program will be used to create on the screen the printed words that the students use to tell about their field trip to the fire station. The teacher explains that she can write down the words they give her in their story more rapidly using the microcomputer. She points out that the letters will not be as large as usual because the screen is smaller than the flipchart page of paper. However, there is an advantage because when they are through composing their story, she can have the printer make copies for everyone in the class. Later, while the story is being printed for each of the children, the teacher explains to the parent who has been visiting the class that this is a reading class engaged in what is called the Language Experience approach to teaching reading. The printing of the eight-line story takes seven minutes to produce 25 copies, one for each child, one for the teacher, and one for the principal.

SETTING: The music teacher explains the day's activity to a fourth grade class during their weekly music period in an urban school.

MICROCOMPUTER: An Apple II with a large color television screen is on a rolling cart. Another large television screen connected to the Apple II is mounted on another rolling cart on the other side of the classroom. The music teacher is using the "MusicMaster"[13] program to provide a lesson for the students on identifying musical scales. The Apple II is connected to an Alpha-Synturi keyboard.

ACTIVITY: The 17 students are in their regular seats. The music teacher explains that the microcomputer will play a scale and display the musical notation for the scale on the screen. The students are to identify the scale by its name, the starting note of the scale, and then use the keyboard of the Apple microcomputer to signal their answer. For the first several scales the music teacher asks for class answers and types the answer they give him on the keyboard. Later, the first student to raise a hand is chosen to come up to the Apple keyboard and press the alphabetic key and the # or - sign to indicate a sharp or flat. After 20 minutes, the music teacher has the students take pencil and paper, number their paper from one through ten, and then, after listening carefully, each student is to record which scale has been played in each of ten selections. When the students have finished their quiz, the music teacher has the microcomputer repeat the ten-scale recognition test and display on the screen the name of each scale and the notes in the scale.

SETTING: It is the last period of the day in an eighth grade math class in an inner-city school in Ohio.

MICROCOMPUTER: A TRS-80, Model III, is mounted on a high rolling cart. Although the teacher and students have to stand to use the keyboard, the screen can be viewed from almost anywhere in the room. The classroom is small and the student desks use all of the available floor space.

ACTIVITY: Students respond enthusiastically to the Radio Shack mathematics program.[14] The student called on tells the teacher what to enter on the keyboard. If the answer is correct, the microcomputer lesson continues printing problems on the screen until the class has answered the twenty problems correctly. If the 20 correct answers are given before class time is over, the students can take turns playing a computer game. The student who has volunteered the most correct answers during the lesson will be the first student to have a turn at the keyboard playing the game. The game involves using the four arrow keys and intercepting the invader force. After ten key choices, the winning student gives up the keyboard position to the student who was second in the number of correct answers given. There was time for only six keyboard choices by this girl before the bell rang. The silent concentration and arm waving behavior of the class in the exercise portion of the class period gives way to much verbal coaching to the winning student at the keyboard as to which target to go after and how to do it. The noise level is indicative of the hold the microcomputer game has on the students' imaginations and contrasts markedly with the quiet that marked the exercise segment of the class period.

SETTING: There are four groups of students in a third grade classroom in a small city in South Dakota.

MICROCOMPUTER: There are three Commodore PET microcomputers in a third grade classroom. The PETS are on separate low tables with four or five chairs at each table. The "Distance and Direction"[15] cassette program has been loaded by a parent volunteer into two of the PET microcomputers and the cassette player is connected to the third PET, although the program has been loaded into that microcomputer as well.

ACTIVITY: Part of the class is still working in their reading group with the teacher. The parent volunteer has organized the 14 pupils who are finished with their reading activity into three table groups and has explained that each child will take turns at the keyboard and make choices of direction and distance in response to the microcomputer program they will view on the screen. When the direction chosen is not right, or the distance chosen is inaccurate, the student gets immediate feedback indicating their poor choice by seeing the visual image of their decision play itself out before their eyes on the video screen. The greatest problem for the volunteer parent in assisting with this microcomputer activity is keeping the high spirits of the children from becoming loud voices that intrude on the reading activity on the other side of the room. This computer activity is a reward to three of the reading groups for their previous good performance. Later, the microcomputers will be used by the entire class with a computer program called "Trail West,"[16] a simulation of pioneers on the Oregon Trail to the West that will occupy all of the social studies class period today. Tomorrow another class will have the microcomputers in their classroom for the day.

SETTING: The sixth grade students and their teacher are grouped around five tables in a suburban school in the midwest.

MICROCOMPUTER: Five Apple II+ microcomputers are located on the tables with students occupying six chairs around each table.

ACTIVITY: Each group of six students is busy with a computer simulation program called "Lemonade Stand."[17]

This economic education program involves students in deciding on the price to charge for a glass of lemonade, the number of glasses of lemonade to make, and the number of advertising signs to prepare. Each student competes with the five or six other students in attempting to make the most money selling lemonade. Because the weather and other events that can affect lemonade sales are randomly selected by the microcomputer, there is considerable variation between the results experienced by the individual students. Their respective good fortune and bad luck are evident in the exclamations heard in the classroom. The students are enjoying themselves and do not realize that this exercise is a part of the teacher's response to a state mandated program in career and economic education.

SETTING: The teacher is supervising the use of four microcomputers by 21 children in the second grade of a suburban grade school.

MICROCOMPUTER: Two TRS-80, Model III, and two Apple II+ microcomputers are in use at four low tables. The program being run in all four microcomputers is the "Spell-N-Time"[18] program.

ACTIVITY: The students are working on a spelling program that has been customized by their teacher to present the ten words on this week's spelling list. The program provides scoring of the students' performance, and some rivalry is evident at three of the tables over the extent of improvement in an individual's score over an earlier attempt. An individual's score depends on correctness in spelling each word, achievement of correct spelling on first or second attempt, and on quickness of response. The fourth table has six children, and they evidently have less enthusiasm for the task. The teacher explains to a visitor that this is a unique program in two ways: it is one of the few that encourages teacher input of specifically useful teaching and learning material like this week's spelling list, and it is one of the programs that can be obtained for both the Apple and TRS-80 brands of microcomputer.

SETTING: A Learning Resource Center in a grade school located in a small Arkansas city where seven students from a fifth grade class are working on a special assignment to decide whether a game can be added to a computer program their teacher uses for reading comprehension.

MICROCOMPUTER: One Apple II+ and one TRS-80, Model III, are housed in a two-sided study carrel in the Learning Resource Center of the school.

ACTIVITY: The students have found an article in a microcomputer magazine that gives the code lines for a program called "Kaboom".[19] This is a game that provides a chance to shoot down a ship by pressing the space bar of the microcomputer keyboard as the ship moves back and forth across the screen. The students have already typed in the program code lines on both the Apple and the TRS-80 microcomputer and have satisfied themselves that the program works. Their next task is to add the "Kaboom" program code lines to the reading comprehension program so that when a student gets seven or more of the ten questions right, the student will automatically have a chance to play the "Kaboom" game as a reward. There is considerable discussion on how many attempts to shoot down the passing ship a student should be given as the reward for doing well on the reading comprehension program. The period ends before the seven students finish their task and they agree to meet after school to complete their assignment.

How do you create a favorable teaching and learning climate in your classroom? Perhaps the scenarios provided above will give you some ideas you can transfer or adapt to your situation. The key ingredients seem to be the attitude of the teacher, the availability of microcomputers for student use, and some programs that are relevant to the grade level and subject involved. Moreover, it is worth noting that the teacher is not called upon to know any of the technical aspects of microcomputer operation. What a teacher needs to know about microcomputers and their instructional use is what programs have educational relevance for the grade and subjects being taught and how to use those programs effectively for the best student learning outcomes. One special episode presented above is worth pointing out. That is where seven fifth grade pupils were using their ingenuity to create an addition of a game that would serve as a reward for good performance by fellow students after using a commercial program in reading comprehension. These students, like many today, know more about microcomputers and programming than they may know about English grammar or the rules for long division. A teacher should use their skills and give their self-esteem a boost without fear that somehow having them do some computer programming will threaten the role of the teacher. As they become involved in the preparation of learning materials, they learn too. The climate in which teaching and learning of the most meaningful sort can take place is found in an environment where students and teachers can be partners with a microcomputer in mutual exploration and learning.

NOTE TO THE TEACHER: If you are planning to use any of the Activities in this book, please do yourself the favor of running each Activity you plan to use *before* you expect your students to use and benefit from the activity. Every effort has been made to make sure the lines of program code and other instructions will work as expected on the brands of microcomputers specified; however, things can go wrong, and the authors do not want you to experience the embarrassment of an uncooperative computer in front of your class!

ACTIVITY ONE

MICROCOMPUTERS AND SOCIETY

> *1. OBJECTIVE:*
> The students will identify some of the issues and trends involving the use of microcomputers and computers and their impact on society.

2. TEACHER PREPARATION:
Refer to the section of Chapter one entitled Computers and Society. In addition to the suggested questions for discussion in the text, create a list of any local issues that your students may have heard or read about. Divide the class into groups of three to five students. Assign a question, trend, or issue to each small group of students for their discussion. Each group will report their findings to the entire class.

3. STUDENT INSTRUCTIONS:
Each student should interact with others in the group by contributing to the discussion when considering the question. Encourage discussion between groups on each report as it is given.

ACTIVITY TWO

MICROCOMPUTER FAMILIARIZATION I

1. OBJECTIVE:
The students will be able to locate the letters of the alphabet on the microcomputer keyboard.

2. TEACHER PREPARATION:
Mark each of the keyboard symbols appropriate to your brand of microcomputer on 3 × 5 cards. Put the cards on a bulletin board in the correct position for your microcomputer keyboard. Have your students make a copy of your keyboard arrangement on lined paper. You may want them to copy just one row of letters, numbers, or symbols in a single session. Have students practice with their paper copy of the keyboard. When students have demonstrated familiarity with their hand lettered keyboards, you can have them use the microcomputer keyboard.

3. STUDENT INSTRUCTIONS:
Now that you have used your own hand-lettered paper

keyboard for practice, try typing the following letters with your left hand.

A   D   R   T   W   X   B   Q   V   Z   E   S   F

What two letters for the left hand were left out? Now try typing the following letters and symbols with your right hand.

Y   K   O   P   M   N   U   H   J   I   ,   /

What keys for the right hand were you *not* asked to type?

LOGO ALTERNATIVE

1. OBJECTIVE:
The student will be able to locate the keys on the keyboard needed to use LOGO.

2. TEACHER PREPARATION:
Mark each of the keyboard letters, numbers, and symbols used in LOGO that are appropriate for your brand of microcomputer on 3×5 cards. Put the cards on the bulletin board in the correct position for your microcomputer keyboard. Have your students make a copy of the keyboard arrangement on lined paper. You may want them to copy just one row of letters, numbers, or symbols in a single session. When they have completed hand lettering their copy of the keys for LOGO in the correct keyboard location, you will want to demonstrate to students how their fingers can reach all of the keys they will need for LOGO. Have students practice with their paper copy of the keyboard. When students have demonstrated familiarity with their hand-lettered keyboards, you can have them use the microcomputer keyboard.

3. STUDENT INSTRUCTIONS:
Now that you have used your own paper keyboard for practice, try typing the following LOGO commands on the microcomputers:

FD30

What happens?

RT45

What happens?

FD20

What happens?

4. NOTE TO TEACHER:
When each student has had a turn at following these instructions, ask one student to type in class suggestions and let them all see what appears on the screen. You don't want to spoil the discovery experience for your students, so limit what *you* suggest the student should type.

ACTIVITY THREE
INFORMATION AGE

1. OBJECTIVE:
The students will be able to describe some of the ways microcomputers are used in school, government, and business.

2. TEACHER PREPARATION:
Provide materials for mounting clippings from newspapers and magazines (i.e., a bulletin board, materials for drawing pictures, and the equipment needed to cut out the articles and pictures the students find).

3. STUDENT INSTRUCTIONS:
Ask your students to bring copies of recent magazines and newspapers to school so they can cut out advertising, articles, pictures, and news stories about computers and microcomputers.

In middle school grades and above, as a variation of this bulletin board approach, you might ask students to report on the advertising on television and TV news stories they see in which computers or microcomputers are used or displayed. The students should keep a record or log of the time, the station, and the kind of computer or microcomputer that was featured.

4. NOTE TO TEACHER:
You may want to keep a scrapbook of newspaper pictures, articles, and advertising printed in the local newspaper or the nearest metropolitan newspaper. One teacher has created a dramatic display of microcomputer advertising that reveals the constantly lower prices being advertised. As of June, 1983, that scrapbook showed the lowest price microcomputer was a 2K Timex-Sinclair at $29.95 in a Sears Roebuck advertisement compared with the original $149.95 price.

ACTIVITY FOUR

MICROCOMPUTER FAMILIARIZATION II

1. OBJECTIVE:
The student will be able to insert a disk in the disk drive of a microcomputer and enter the necessary commands to run the program.

2. TEACHER PREPARATION:
You must have a program disk, such as the Apple DOS 3.3 Disk Master, that has the necessary disk operating system (DOS) recorded on it and at least one program that will provide the student with some experience with CAI. The program "Animals" on the Apple DOS 3.3 Disk Master would be a good choice. However, to use this program you must make a copy of the "Animals" program on another disk. Consult your Apple DOS Manual for instructions on using the program named FID to copy "Animals" onto another disk. When that copy has been made, use the newly created disk and the COPYA program from the Apple DOS 3.3 Master Disk to make as many additional

copies as you will need. If you are using another brand of microcomputer, you will need to follow the instructions for that brand and use the disk resources you have for that microcomputer.

If you do not have access to the Apple DOS 3.3 Master Disk with the "Animals" program or other CAI program is disk, cassette, or cartridge, you can give your students a beginning experience with a CAI program by typing in the lines of code of a published program. One source for these program code lines is found in the microcomputer magazines that pertain to your brand of microcomputer. You can improvise a CAI program by typing in the following lines of BASIC code that will work in almost every microcomputer brand.

10   PRINT "WHAT IS YOUR AGE"
20   INPUT A
30   PRINT "HOW OLD WILL YOU BE WHEN YOU ARE TWICE AS OLD AS YOU ARE NOW"
40   INPUT B
50   IF B <> A*2 THEN PRINT "TRY AGAIN!": GOTO 30
60   IF B = A*2 THEN PRINT "YOU ARE RIGHT!"
70   END

If you use these code lines, please realize that you can change the words within the quotation marks so they are more suitable for your students. Check lines 50 and 60 in your program to make sure the arithmetic calculations agree with the story problem you are using.

3. STUDENT INSTRUCTIONS:
Give students directions on (a) how to insert the disk in the disk drive and (b) the keyboard commands to bring the "Animals" program onto the screen (type in RUN ANIMALS and press RETURN). You will need to stress the importance of reading the messages on the screen,

typing in the required answers carefully, and then pressing the RETURN key. You should give your students a time limit for running this program.

ACTIVITY FIVE

MICROCOMPUTER FAMILIARIZATION III

1. OBJECTIVE:
The student will be able to program a dialogue with the microcomputer using the PRINT and INPUT commands.

2. TEACHER PREPARATION:
Write on the board:

10   PRINT "HELLO, WHAT IS YOUR NAME"

20   INPUT N$

30   PRINT "HELLO, "N$" HOW ARE YOU FEELING"

40   INPUT H$

Have students copy the four lines on notebook paper. Suggest the reason why (a) the line numbers are spaced at intervals of ten, (b) the microcomputer must be given the words to print and these words must be enclosed in quotation marks, (c) the input statement in lines 20 and 40 are used, (d) one variable was called N$ and the other variable was called H$, and (e) a space is needed after the comma following HELLO and another space is needed between the third quotation mark and the word HOW.

3. STUDENT INSTRUCTIONS:
Type the program you have copied in your notebook on the microcomputer keyboard. Add at least two more lines (of BASIC code) in the form of another question to be asked by the microcomputer and another answer to be

accepted. Then RUN the program. (If your program does not RUN properly, check your program code lines for errors.)

ACTIVITY SIX
MICROCOMPUTER FAMILIARIZATION IV

1. OBJECTIVE:
The students will be able to type in the commands that cause the microcomputer to begin an infinite loop and then stop the looping process.

2. TEACHER PREPARATION:
Write on the board:

```
10  PRINT "WHAT IS YOUR NAME"
20  INPUT N$
30  PRINT "WHAT IS YOUR FAVORITE
       SUBJECT IN SCHOOL"
40  INPUT L$
50  PRINT N$ " LIKES " L$ " BEST."
60  GOTO 50
```

Note that in line 50 the spaces after the quotation mark in front of LIKES, the space after LIKES in front of the quotation mark, and the space after the third quotation mark in front of BEST are important to provide a readable screen image. To stop the constant repeating caused by line 60, the student will use the following keys, depending on the brand of microcomputer: on the Commodore, press RUN/STOP key; on the Apple, press both CTRL and C keys; on the TRS-80, press BREAK key.

3. STUDENT INSTRUCTIONS:
You are to copy the program lines from the board onto lined paper. Then type the program on the microcomputer keyboard. Read each line carefully as it appears on the

> screen to make certain you entered the program correctly. After you have typed all the code lines, type RUN and press the ENTER or RETURN key. Answer the questions the microcomputer asks you and press ENTER or RETURN after each answer. Your teacher will tell you how to stop the constant repeating of the message on the screen, which is caused by a "loop" in the programming logic. Although loops are sometimes useful, you don't always want them in a microcomputer program.

ACTIVITY SEVEN

MICROCOMPUTER FAMILIARIZATION V

1. OBJECTIVE:
The students will be able to solve some arithmetic problems using the microcomputer to do the calculating.

2. TEACHER PREPARATION:
The students will need instructions about the symbols the microcomputer uses to add, subtract, multiply, and divide. These symbols are usually +, -, *, and /, respectively. The program can be as simple as:

    10   PRINT 10/5

or

    20   PRINT 2 + 3 + 4 + 8

Line 10 will yield the answer 2, which is all that will appear on the screen. Line 20 will yield the answer 17, and again that is all that will appear on the screen. To get a more complete statement of the arithmetic process with the answer, you will need to give the students the following form of the line 10 and line 20.

    10   PRINT "WHAT IS THE ANSWER IF YOU DIVIDE 10 BY 5?" 10/5

and

> 20 PRINT "WHAT IS THE SUM OF 2 PLUS 3 PLUS 4 PLUS 8?" 2+3+4+8

Write on the board the same kind of examples as given above, but appropriate to the level and topic for the day.

3. STUDENT INSTRUCTIONS:
You are to solve two of your arithmetic problems using the microcomputer. To do so, you must write the program line you plan to type on the keyboard of the microcomputer. Follow the examples you have been given on the board. When you think you have a correctly written line, type it on the microcomputer keyboard. Check to make sure you typed it correctly. Then type RUN and press the RETURN or ENTER key.

ACTIVITY EIGHT

MICROCOMPUTER FAMILIARIZATION VI

1. OBJECTIVE:
The students will be able to format or initialize a disk on which they can save programs they create in the class.

2. TEACHER PREPARATION:
This is an activity useful only in those classes in which the microcomputer is equipped with one or more disk drives. Arrangements will have to be made for the purchase of a blank disk by each student, or the provision of a blank disk for each student by the school. This activity is most useful if there is an opportunity for students to save a copy of something they have created on the microcomputer. The

Apple and the TRS-80 system requirements and commands are:

Brand	Required	Action Required
Apple	DOS 3.3 Disk Master	Turn on micro. When you see prompt, INSERT Blank disk, type INIT NAME and press RETURN. When you see prompt, type CATALOG and press RETURN to verify that you have initialized the disk.
TRS-80	TRSDOS disk	Turn on micro. When you see that TRSDOS is ready; type FORMAT and press ENTER.

Answer the "which drive" question and press ENTER and place a blank disk in that drive. Answer the "name of disk" question with your choice of 8 letters or less, and the "password" question with PASSWORD. After pressing ENTER, wait for the completion of the formatting process. To verify that you have created a usable disk type DIR and press ENTER.

In typing either CATALOG or DIR, students should see the name they gave the disk appear on the screen.

3. STUDENT INSTRUCTIONS:

Follow the instructions provided by your teacher to create a disk that will permit you to save programs that you write and word processing files that you create. After saving a program on a disk, you can later RUN that program on the microcomputer. Your disk has been initialized or formatted so that it has a magnetic track on which the microcomputer can record the programs or word processing files you create. Your disk has neither an "operating system" nor a "word-processing program" and thus can only be used when you have used a "system" disk when you first turn on the microcomputer. A system disk tells the microcomputer how to receive and manipulate input.

NOTES

1. "Civil War," "Sell Apples," "Sell Bicycles," and "Sell Plants" are part of *Elementary—Volume 3, Social Studies* (Grades 3-8); "Fish," "Minerals," and "Odell Lake" are part of *Science—Volume 3* (Junior and Senior High School); "Furs," "Nomad," "Oregon," and "Voyageur" are part of *Elementary—Volume 6* (Grades 5-7). In: Microcomputer Courseware Catalog. St. Paul, MN: Minnesota Educational Computing Consortium, 1982.
2. From description of "Community Search." In: The Search Series. New York: Webster Division, McGraw-Hill Book Company, 1982, p. 1.
3. From description of "Getting Ready to Read and Add." In: Quality Courseware. Crystal Lake, IL: Follett Library Book Co., 1982, p. 40.
4. From description of "Using Verbs." In: Lakeshore Curriculum Materials. Carson, California: Lakeshore Curriculum Materials Co., 1983, p. 160.
5. From description of "Power Processing Programs." In: Reading, Listening, Learning Resource Catalog. Huntington Station, New York: Instructional/Communications Technology, Inc., 1982, p. 80.
6. From description of "Problem Solving in Algebra." In: Britannica Computer Based Learning. Chicago: Encyclopaedia Britannica Educational Corporation, 1982, p. 6.
7. From description of "Sentence Combining." In: Turning Computer Systems Into Learning Systems. St. Louis, MO: Milliken Publishing Company, 1982, p. 3.
8. From description of "Course Manager." In: Texas Instruments Home Computer Program Library. Ft. Worth: Texas Instruments Incorporated, 1982, p. 10.
9. From description of "Direction and Distance." In: Microcomputer Instructional Materials. Englewood Cliffs, NJ: Scholastic, Inc., 1982, p. 31.
10. From description of "Tutorial Problem Solving in Math." In: Microcomputer Courseware Catalog. Westminster, Maryland: Random House School Division, 1982, p. 18.
11. "Reading Is Fun." Glenview, IL: Scott, Foresman and Company, 1982.
12. "The Bank Street Writer." New York, NY: Scholastic, Inc., 1982.
13. "Music Master I." Palo Alto, CA: Syntauri Corporation, 1982.
14. "K-8 Math Program," Vol. I. Ft. Worth, TX: Radio Shack Division of Tandy Corporation, 1980.

15. "Distance and Direction." Minneapolis, MN: Micro-Ed Incorporated, 1980.
16. "Trail West." Minneapolis, MN: Micro-Ed Incorporated, 1980.
17. "Lemonade." Cupertino, CA: Apple Computer Company, 1980.
18. "Spell-N-Time." Fresno, CA: School and Home CourseWare, Inc., 1980.
19. Koetke W. Learning with spaceships. *Microcomputing.* October, 1981, pp. 18–21.

2
MICROCOMPUTER SOFTWARE

This chapter identifies some teaching and learning activities that are enhanced by using a microcomputer and the appropriate software. The background needed to evaluate the software available for a given brand of microcomputer is included in the following specific topics:
- Selecting teaching and learning activities—drill, problem solving, tutorial, simulation and programming in LOGO, PILOT, and BASIC as computer control techniques
- Courseware or program sources
- Criteria for software selection
- Ease of customizing programs
- Graphics—sound and color factors in program selection

Each topic is expanded by the reasons for classroom instructional use. In addition, a list of Recommended Readings and Media for further learning and Learning Activities for students are provided.

TEACHING AND LEARNING MICROCOMPUTER PROGRAMS

One of the most important ideas involved in using a microcomputer as an instructional tool is implicit in the concept that it is only a tool. The microcomputer does not change any of the instructional priorities of a teacher. The teaching strategies employed in a classroom will be changed only slightly, if at all, by the use of a microcomputer. For example, drill becomes more palatable to both teacher and students and, thus, will be more conscientiously used when it is educationally valid. In like manner, problem solving moves ahead more expeditiously when the problem can be individually addressed by a student without involving the entire class. A possible addition to the curriculum after the arrival of a microcomputer might be to use LOGO, PILOT, or BASIC programming languages as a means of giving instructions to the computer to solve problems; this conveys to the student a sense of control over the microcomputer. In the typical choices required of a student in CAI software or courseware, students often experience a feeling of being controlled by the microcomputer and its CAI program, and to a large extent, the student is controlled.

WHY USE DRILL COURSEWARE?

Drill and practice have been a much maligned element in the school routine. This is because teachers are not comfortable with the role of taskmaster and with the need to insist on correct outcomes before the student moves on to other learning activities. There was a period of time when learning number concepts, word meanings, correct spelling, and similar components of basic skills was an expected part of every child's school experience. Parents knew and accepted this; teachers and students alike worked to this end. For whatever reasons, the routine in most classrooms across the country moved away from mastery of skills to the point where there is today an active and vocal "back to basics" movement. One of these organizations, The Council for Basic Skill Education (COBSE),[1] has particularly opposed the introduction of microcomputers into schools, viewing the microcomputer as a threat to the emphasis they seek on learning basic skills. What COBSE has overlooked in their zeal for education in basic skills is that a microcomputer is an especially effective tool by which to insist on real mastery of drill material. The microcomputer does not know that the child typing on its keyboard is an adorable fourth grader whose winning smile has been more important in the recorded academic progress than mastery of the material in a lesson. The microcomputer does not know and cannot discriminate against any user because of color, religion, gender, or age.

Some critics of drill object to using a microcomputer drill and practice as "nothing more than a page turning program." Such criticism overlooks the fact that, unlike a print form of drill or practice work, the page represented by the microcomputer screen in a well-constructed program cannot be "turned" until the correct answers have been entered. Many of these microcomputer drill programs provide not only for "turning the page" to the next learning segment, but for jumping the student ahead or branching the student back to a more elementary level of practice and drill. The most highly recommended microcomputer drill-and-practice courseware records a student's performance by reporting not only the number of right and wrong answers but also the specific wrong answers given, and the time it has taken the student to respond. A number of microcomputer drill programs automatically save a record of correct and incorrect student responses. Teachers must analyze the microcomputer record for each student to determine what mistakes are being made and why. Teacher intervention is frequently needed to clarify concepts before additional microcomputer drill and practice is used.

Almost every teacher has observed students who aimlessly page through workbooks without focusing on the print before their eyes. Microcomputers encourage student involvement in some drill-and-practice interaction programs by their gamelike format, the immediate feedback they provide, and the high percentage of success the student experiences because these programs are targeted at the student's level of achievement. The motivation for the student to succeed is higher than any worksheet or flash-card approach can achieve because the microcomputer can give the student the sense of personal attention that a teacher cannot find the time to provide in one-on-one drill. Nor does the teacher have the patience or ability to adjust and keep score as efficiently and untiringly as the microcomputer. Most of the microcomputer drill programs from quality publishers provide for more than one chance for a correct response. Most of these programs also allow the teacher to choose the number of responses the student may give before the microcomputer gives the correct answer to the student user. More useful drill-and-practice programs will give students help in leading them to choose correct answers after they have made a wrong choice.

The microcomputer as a medium for providing students with effective drill fulfills the prediction of B.F. Skinner that machines have the energy and patience needed for simple drill and practice and that "these are all functions that should never have been served by teachers in the first place."[2]

Where drill is part of the educational priority of a school, the microcomputer and the courseware already available can play an important role in improving educational outcomes.

WHY USE PROBLEM-SOLVING COURSEWARE?

Although problem-solving programs are less frequently encountered than drill-and-practice materials for most microcomputers, they are worth finding and using with students. Problem-solving courseware provides the teacher with an opportunity to productively engage the attention of a single student or groups of students with the challenge of solving a problem. Very good problem-solving situations can be organized with two to four students working together in making decisions to solve a problem. This atmosphere also removes the fear some people have of the computer's dehumanization of children. Students have the opportunity to find an answer on their own and to realize mastery of a problem. It is difficult to overstate the potential for improved self-image that such learning success makes. The teacher who cares about individualizing instruction finds problem-solving courseware an especially valuable tool in developing the logical thinking process of students. Using problem solving with individuals or small groups of students often calls for some change in the pattern of the school class period. However, if individualized instruction has been one of the school's priorities, the use of a microcomputer for the implementation of individualized and independent study should fit easily into the teaching and learning process.

Teachers who have used microcomputers in conjunction with their classroom teaching suggest that problem-solving courseware does not have to involve arithmetic problems. One program about which teachers have been enthusiastic involves elementary students in deciding on the direction and distance needed for one object on the screen to intersect with another object. Still another program calls for making a selection of colors so that no part of any two geometric shapes will share a common side that is the same color. Some students solve these problems with careful and extensive thinking and planning, others use trial-and-error methods. In any case, the students discover that finding an answer to a problem can be stimulating and even fun.

The frequent complaint of the adult world is that graduates of many schools do not know methods for problem solving. As students are exposed to microcomputer problem-solving experiences, the complaint could become less frequent. As students solve problems with a microcomputer, higher level thinking becomes challenging and fun.

WHY USE TUTORIAL COURSEWARE?

The idea behind tutorial courseware is that it provides original instruction or reinforcing instruction in a given subject matter. This is an advantage to the teacher and to the student because those students who need extra help can find this help in a computer tutorial program, thus freeing the teacher to work with other students. At times like these, the microcomputer becomes a teacher aide. In addition, with the student absentee problem faced by many schools, the idea of using tutorial microcomputer programs to provide make-up instruction for students who have missed the original session is appealing to many teachers. Teachers often observe that students who are weak in their learning skills are also the students most frequently absent. It does not matter whether the absences cause the weakness in learning skills, or whether weak learning skills predispose the child to miss school whenever possible.

A microcomputer tutorial lesson provides patient and consistent follow-through so that children are taught the material they earlier missed. In addition, some students need reinforcement of instruction given in class before they can successfully practice a skill and then master that skill. A microcomputer tutorial program could provide this service.

A major problem is integrating the microcomputer lesson accurately with the pages of textbook learning that was originally experienced by the class during a student's absence. However, courseware programs are available in which each lesson has been cross-referenced with many of the most popular textbook series. In the Materials Resource list, you will find a reference to several programs that provide a cross-reference that correlates the microcomputer lessons with specific chapters and pages in popular textbooks.

Publishers of widely used textbooks in both elementary and secondary schools need to have teacher and educational administrator encouragement to provide appropriate microcomputer counterparts to textbooks in all subject areas. When providing this supplementary courseware, it will be helpful to the teacher if the scope and sequence of lesson materials is clearly set forth in the courseware documentation.

WHY USE SIMULATION COURSEWARE?

Simulation may not have been accorded as much of the classroom day, nor as high an educational priority in the instructional plans in the past, as will now seem appropriate and desirable. Simulations can take several forms. In the past, most print simulations were limited to some form of storytelling scenario that offered a series of choices, the consequences of which could be learned by turning to the page the reader was told to read next in a programmed learning book. A number of effective scenarios were available when the computer time-sharing mode was used. The choices entered on the computer terminal generated a response from the mainframe computer as to the outcome of the choice that was made. In both situations, the costs and related benefits did not give simulation a very high priority in most school curricula. A higher priority position and time requirement will obviously require changes in a school curriculum and its implemen-

Using simulation courseware.

tation. Simulations have not been widely available in print format. However, large computer simulations for science and some social studies classes have been successful where a school district could afford the costs of this service. With the advent of the microcomputer, earlier wisdom about the cost versus benefit balance has been changed. Simulations are now a cost effective way to communicate a number of insights about science, history, and other subject matter that could not have been considered economically possible before. Simulations are a significant part of the courseware available from cooperative organizations such as the Minnesota Educational Computer Consortium (MECC). Probably more young students have been exposed to their first notion of economics from using the MECC "Lemonade Stand"[3] simulation than any other learning experience. Another widely used type of simulation involves the westward movement of American pioneers, called "Oregon."[4] Still another popular simulation involves the MECC program "Odell Lake,"[5] in which an understanding of a life chain can be observed by children as they watch the predatory behaviors of larger and smaller fish in the food chain. The variety of simulation programs available for use is improving. The decision by organizations such as CONDUIT at Iowa City, Iowa, and Control Data Corporation to make their computer series of programs available in microcomputer format is indicative of the importance attached to serving the classroom market.

WAYS TO USE LOGO, PILOT, AND BASIC PROGRAMMING RESOURCES

The most challenging aspect of using microcomputers in the classroom is how far to go in giving students experience with programming the microcomputer. Teachers who have used microcomputer courseware in their classrooms often report that the typical CAI program leaves the student feeling that they are controlled by the microcomputer. Although such control may be the mark of a very good program in CAI, the

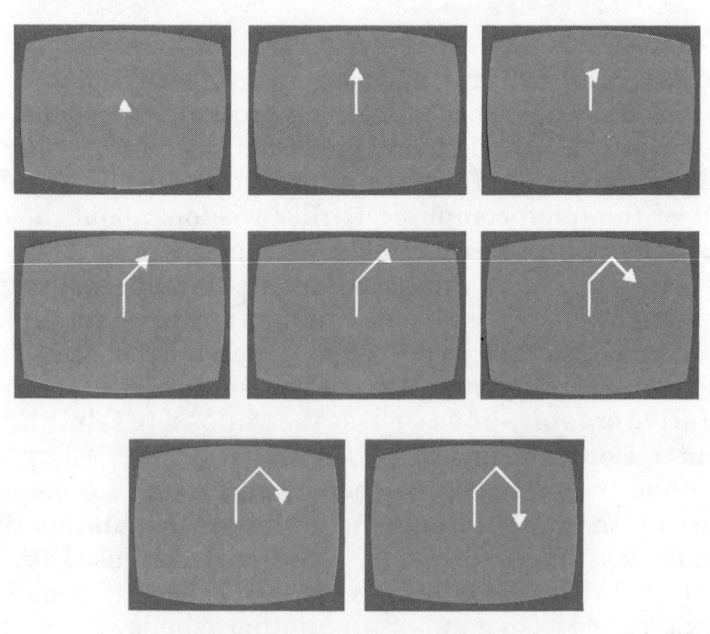

Movement of the LOGO turtle.

question is raised, "Should the computer be used to program the child or should the child program the computer?" With the advent of LOGO, it became possible to use a microcomputer programming language with even the young child in a preschool setting. The following list of benefits of LOGO for children at a preoperational level of cognitive development is worth examining. LOGO makes possible

- Number, letter, and color recognition
- Symbol association
- Directionality
- Decision making
- Following instructions
- Memory recall
- Spatial awareness
- Sequential thinking
- Creativity
- Computer awareness

There can be a substantial gap between what is possible and what is achieved. The work of Papert and others who have worked with preschool children suggests that a number of developmental learning tasks can be assisted by exposure to LOGO in using a microcomputer. The list given above is a realistic recital of gains that very young children can achieve. However, there are teachers who object to such young children having control of their environment, let alone control of a microcomputer. Note that the list assumes the child is encouraged to use both the "Turtle Graphics"[6] mode of LOGO, and the "Sprite"[7] mode to the extent that the child can accept this beginning programming challenge.

With a primary school child who has used LOGO, teachers report benefits such as (1) more positive self-image, (2) attention to detail, (3) a capacity for both divergent and logical thinking, (4) improved decision-making skills, (5) better spelling, math, and communication skills, and (6) awareness of the computer as a tool.

In addition, LOGO becomes a bridge to the learning of more advanced languages and concepts that will be useful in the "information age." These advantages are important to children at both ends of the spectrum of exceptional children, to the gifted as well as to the educationally handicapped.

PILOT has been the special province of middle school and junior high school teachers who express enthusiasm about using this simple language as a means of involving their students in the experience of controlling the microcomputer by creating simple programs in almost any subject field. The eight commands used in PILOT can be taught in a single class period and students can begin to create their own programs in the days that follow. When students in junior high school have the use of microcomputers for two or three weeks, the experience these students have in creating their own programs, seeing them run, and (when a printer is available) being able to take them home in printed form, makes them converts to the heady joys of microcomputer use.

Like LOGO, Pascal is a newcomer to the programming language field. It is the product of work done at the University of California, San Diego, and features a structured approach to building each element of a program. Pascal has made considerable headway for a new programming language. It is now the computer programming language in which secondary students can gain advanced credit toward college requirements through the Educational Testing Service by taking an advanced placement examination.

BASIC as a programming language has been available ever since 1967, when this language was created by Kemeny and Kurtz of Dartmouth College. In the past several years, a new approach to using BASIC as a programming language has emerged. It is grounded in the best traditions of the discovery method and assumes that the student will want to experiment with the language to achieve goals unique to that student's purposes. Such an approach typically consists of five components at each level in a series of creative programming that becomes more difficult at each level of achievement. The five segments of one creative programming approach are:[8]

- The first segment consists of instructions, examples, exercises, and recall experiences. Programming commands in BASIC are learned at this level. Ways in which these commands can be logically organized and used are presented.
- The second segment consists of mini-challenges, projects that require sequential organization, creativity, good

logical thinking, and sticking with a problem until it is solved.
- The third segment consists of students' playing computer games. These are games that call for hand-eye coordination, shape discrimination, cause-effect relationships, improved reaction time, following directions, increased attention span, improved spatial relations, and organizing a game winning strategy.
- The fourth segment consists of problems much like those encountered in real life. The student is encouraged to undertake the programming in BASIC that will solve a problem.
- The fifth segment consists of encouraging the student to use the microcomputer as a tool to serve the student's needs in any way that seems important to the student.

Those who have observed the program described above report that it is especially effective with gifted children. The effectiveness of the approach is apparently not limited to children; many adults have undertaken this type of creative programming approach with high success.

The reader may encounter schools where BASIC is still taught in its traditional form. This means teaching students to create a program that will calculate the solution to a mathematic, scientific, or business problem. The mathematic, scientific, and business applications of BASIC are of little interest to many students. The development of a focus on BASIC that asserts that the language can be used in the pursuit of many other goals therefore appears desirable.

The learning opportunities represented by the availability of LOGO, PILOT, and the special approaches to BASIC programming will need to be faced by every teacher who has the good fortune to have a microcomputer available for student use. Some teachers will want to explore Pascal as a programming language. The availability of these programming approaches raises the issue of what objectives are appropriate to teaching any programming language. Is the teaching of programming meant to produce programs and potential programmers, or is such teaching meant to produce more self-confident and logical thinking students for the information age?

44   *Microcomputer Software*

Getting to know BASIC.

COURSEWARE OR PROGRAM SOURCES

Some teachers may be used to having a curriculum specialist provide most of the instructional materials for classroom use or to having a publisher's representative call and leave sample books. However, this assistance in finding instructional material may not be available in your school district. Teachers are often faced with the need to find quality educational programs or courseware for a microcomputer. The six major sources to explore for microcomputer courseware are:

- Microcomputer manufacturers
- Major publishing companies
- Microcomputer software distributors
- Computer magazines and education journals
- Cottage industry advertisements in magazines
- Local computer stores
- Computer clubs and user groups

There will probably be an increase in the importance of major publishing companies and microcomputer manufacturers as sources for courseware in the coming decade. The impact of cottage-industry entrepreneurs will probably decrease, whereas the importance of local computer stores and computer software distributors will probably remain unchanged.

Microcomputer manufacturers vary in the number of educational software choices available for classroom use. Texas Instruments has a catalog that is available on request, but an interested teacher will have to phone or write the Texas headquarters for a copy. Radio Shack has a catalog that is widely available through both its computer stores and departments, as well as at regular Radio Shack stores. Apple's directory has over 400 pages of available programs. Commodore makes available over 600 programs in the public domain, fully copyable without concern for copyright requirements. The attention of microcomputer manufacturers has increasingly been turned to creating a series of courseware, much like a textbook series. One of the problems of depending on microcomputer manufacturers for special information about their educational courseware is that they do not have traveling representatives.

Book publishing companies still have traveling representatives, although the electronic publishing division of the book company is often not represented by these representatives. Book publishers have experienced problems in creating sufficient knowledge and enthusiasm on the part of their representatives and thus have given the microcomputer assignment to others. As is the case with the microcomputer manufacturers, there tend to be too few of the publisher representatives in their electronic publishing divisions to call on many schools.

Microcomputer software distributors are a new source of information for teachers and curriculum specialists. Some of these distributors offer a money-back guarantee, as do some book publishers. There are still some distributors who accept orders only when the buyer has adequate corporate credentials or a valid VISA or MasterCard. Teachers who want to buy courseware from microcomputer distributors should inquire about whether a school purchase order will be accepted.

It is necessary to read microcomputer magazines and educational journals for their microcomputer courseware reviews and for the cottage-industry advertising if you want to keep up-to-date about microcomputers and compatible software. This monthly reading is much more work than teachers, or even curriculum specialists, usually have time to do.

A convenient source of programs for typical teachers is the local computer store where they are able to try a program before it is purchased. In selecting any courseware, it is important to run the program before buying it. This is also true of highly recommended software you have seen reviewed in educational journals. Software programs that are highly recommended in evaluation reviews may not fit your teaching needs. Another source of information about microcomputer programs are other teachers who use microcomputers in the classroom. Checking with people who are already using programs is an excellent way of determining the usefulness of software.

CRITERIA FOR SOFTWARE SELECTION

There is no single standard for courseware evaluation and selection. This may be as it should be. Not everyone evaluates a new text for adoption with a single set of standards. However, teachers report a degree of confusion over the rival claims of various organizations and writers about the desirability of one set of evaluation criteria over another. The principal resources for teacher consideration are given in the Materials Resource list and also in the Recommended Reading and Media listing.

The Microsift evaluation format of the Northwest Regional Educational Laboratory at Portland, Oregon calls for rating educational software on the basis of the 21 factors listed below.

EXAMPLE

- Content accuracy
- Educational value
- Lack of cultural stereotyping
- Well-defined objectives
- Accomplishment of stated objectives
- Clarity of presentation
- Appropriateness of difficulty level
- Appropriateness of color, sound, and graphics
- Appropriateness of motivational level
- Challenge to student creativity
- Effectiveness of feedback employed
- Student control of format
- Integrative appropriateness or prior learning
- Generalization capability of content
- Comprehensiveness of program
- Adequacy of packaging
- Effectiveness of information displays
- Clarity of instructions
- Teacher facility and ease with program
- Appropriateness to computer technology
- Reliability of program

These listed factors cover most of the elements of good teaching materials and presentation. A recent article in *Educational Computer Magazine*,[9] presents the idea that evaluation instruments often lack a theory base. The evaluation instruments generally available tend to treat all learning tasks alike. Too often, the learning environment is not considered when evaluating courseware. A useful distinction is made by the National Council of Teachers of Mathematics (NCTM)[10] in their approach to evaluating computerized instructional materials. Their presentation of a software evaluation checklist and a sample software documentation sheet represents an effective division of the subject matter into components that can be considered by the classroom teacher. The NCTM suggestions are equally applicable to all subjects.

Some of the most important criteria in terms of school use are ignored by each of the preceding approaches. For example, neither the list of Microsift's 21 factors nor the NCTM listing gives any attention to whether the proposed microcomputer program has any place in the curriculum. Nor does either list consider "backup-copy" policy. Only the NCTM approach considers costs per disk or specific hardware or software required.

The teacher not already familiar with software evaluation should obtain and study the Recommended Readings and Media on software evaluation. Some school districts may want to follow the same pattern in piloting a software program as they use when piloting a new textbook series.

EASE OF CUSTOMIZING SOFTWARE

Suppose that you have found a courseware program that passes each and every test, every evaluation criteria, with flying colors. You would really like to use this software program to individualize instruction for students. You discover that nowhere in your evaluation approach have you considered whether and how easily you can customize the program. For example, when using vocabulary or spelling software programs, the teacher may want to update the spelling or vocabulary list daily, or to increase or decrease the number of words presented in each lesson. Teachers who want to customize a program in this way may find that because the program has been "locked," there is no chance to examine the program code lines and enter new words in a spelling exercise. Software producers engage in locking a program to prevent its copying. Copying clearly violates copyright law when it is done to avoid buying additional disk programs, thus depriving the software creator of income from the sale of further disks. Copying for archival purposes is not a breach of copyright law, but locking a program prevents creating a backup copy. It also makes it impossible for a teacher to change any program lines of code. Where program code lines of a courseware program can be listed on the screen of the microcomputer, it is not difficult to change the DATA lines. These DATA lines contain the words and phrases that provide the pool of content material selected by the randomizing command in the program. Thus, the words of a spelling lesson particularly appropriate to your classroom at a given time can be inserted in place of the spelling words that are listed in the DATA lines of the program as it is delivered to your school. The ability to list DATA lines makes possible one kind of customizing that may be desirable in adapting the program to a specific class use.

GRAPHICS, SOUND, AND COLOR
FACTORS IN PROGRAM SELECTION

Part of the drama that captivates teachers and students in any microcomputer lesson presentation are the graphic, sound, and color elements found in many software programs. This capability of the microcomputer alternately has been praised and ridiculed. The praise is obviously self-serving in some advertising that would lead the reader to think that only those programs with graphics, sound, and color are effective at holding youngsters' attention. Similarly, the ridicule can be self-serving on the part of those school systems that have adopted a microcomputer brand where color, for example, is difficult to achieve. Probably, there are no popular microcomputer brands where graphics, sound, and color cannot be achieved in some way.

Graphics in varying degrees of sharpness and resolution can be achieved on every microcomputer used in education. High-resolution graphics may be important to some subject matter, and certainly will be more important to some teachers than to other teachers. The authoring systems described in

Chapter three provide for graphic presentation that can be interspersed with text and questions. Some of the PILOT language systems provide for creation of graphics. Every version of BASIC used in the brands of microcomputers that are used in schools can create graphic screen output, although with some programming difficulty. Graphic printer output can be achieved on many of the printers popular in schools. The extent of graphics use in courseware varies from incidental to heavy. Courseware concerned with some of the sciences will need to use graphic images to a greater extent than courseware for other subjects. If, as the old saying goes, a picture is worth 1,000 words, there is a place for graphics in courseware in almost every subject. A special strength of graphic presentation on a microcomputer in an instructional microcomputer lesson is that the image can be animated. Thus, high-resolution graphics in a demonstration of an engine can show a piston moving as the valves open and close. This is a capability that print illustrations have always lacked.

Sound output from a microcomputer program is almost as easily achieved as graphic presentations on all brands of microcomputers used in schools today. Some microcomputers have a built-in speaker, whereas others require the connection of an external speaker to the cassette port of the microcomputer. Some microcomputers have a wider range of musical tones than others. Earphones can be used with some microcomputers. This is important in a classroom or learning center where extraneous sounds might disturb other students. From an educational standpoint, there are some subjects, such as music and reading, where sound is a distinct advantage. In many fields, however, sound may create more distraction than encouragement. Teachers are urged to check on the possibility of turning off sound as they preview or evaluate programs for classroom use.

Color is an issue that arouses bitter debate. The microcomputers that support color screen output are praised by their owners as the only way to go. The owners of microcomputers that do not originally support color screen output tend to downplay the usefulness of color. Teachers concerned with math and reading, especially with students in middle school grade levels and above report doubts about the use of color. Teachers of primary grades report that children are used to color television and that these children adapt more easily to a microcomputer screen that seems like the TV screen they are used to viewing. In addition, teachers in some urban schools report that color screen capability seems to attract and hold the attention of students who otherwise have short attention spans.

An interesting sidelight on the issue of color is that when the Franklin Ace microcomputer was introduced as the look-alike to the Apple II+, there was no color capability in the unit. Within a short time, an under-50-dollar add-on became available that conferred color screen capability to the Franklin Ace. All Franklin Ace units shipped since December, 1982, have had a built-in color capability. The TRS-80, Model I, likewise had no color capability to begin with until an add-on was created. There are now at least two add-on units called Color-Graf[11] and CHROMAtrs,[12] respectively, providing color screen capability for both the Model I and Model III. The Radio Shack Color Computer and the MC10 model now represent Radio Shack's response to the desire for a microcomputer with color screen capabilities. The effectiveness of color in instruction is yet to be determined, as are the extent and degree to which color is effective in CAI.

SUMMARY

You have been exposed to ideas in this chapter that should encourage effective use of a microcomputer in your teaching. The important point about the several pages devoted to considering Drill, Problem Solving, Tutorial, Simulation, and using LOGO, PILOT, and other programming languages in your teaching is that you and only you can decide what fits your style of classroom presentation. Teachers often return to the classroom from a microcomputer workshop fired with enthusiasm about this new teaching approach and then discover that it just doesn't work for them. Use the kind of teaching approach that works for you. Use the microcomputer as a tool that makes your use of a particular teaching approach more effective and less stressful.

This is also true for those sections of the chapter that deal with courseware sources, software selection criteria, customizing programs and using graphics, sound, or color. Only you can know what fits your style best. The advent of the microcomputer in elementary and secondary education will undoubtedly give rise to another rash of conspicuous behavior and keeping-up-with-the-Joneses on the educational scene. If you focus on the needs of your students and how you can best meet those needs with the tools given you, including the microcomputer, then you can be successful in fostering and guiding the learning process.

ACTIVITY ONE

LOGO Discovery

1. OBJECTIVE:
The students will be able to create a geometric shape on the screen that duplicates a shape they have "walked" through in the classroom.

2. TEACHER PREPARATION:
Have students walk in a square (or other geometric shape) in the classroom. Encourage students to talk about what they did and relate it to the corresponding shape. They went forward so many steps, then turned right or left, then walked forward again so many steps, etc.

3. STUDENT INSTRUCTIONS:
Ask students to type on the microcomputer keyboard the directions for the turtle on the screen so that the turtle will form a square similar to the one the students walked through in the classroom. Let them experiment with what happens when they use different combinations of direction and numbers.

ACTIVITY TWO
SIMPLE PROGRAMMING IN BASIC

1. OBJECTIVE:
The student will be able to write a program to solve a simple arithmetic problem of counting using the microcomputer.

2. TEACHER PREPARATION:
Because there are just four code lines to be entered, the time required for programming is very short. The time it takes the microcomputer to count that many numbers and display them on the screen, although much faster than any student can count, will take time. These same four lines of code will run on the Commodore, the Apple, and the TRS-80. Plan on the Apple taking five *minutes* to count to more than 10,500. The count to a million will take about eight hours. It may take longer on some microcomputers. Some teachers have used this activity as a basis for having students estimate when the computer will reach the million mark.

3. STUDENT INSTRUCTIONS:
Enter the following four lines of BASIC code:

```
10  FOR X = 0 TO 1000000
20  PRINT X
30  NEXT X
40  END
RUN
```

Record the exact time the program begins in order to calculate the elapsed time and estimate when the microcomputer will reach one million.

If you want the program to run without printing the numbers on the screen, leave out line 20. When you want to see what would have *just been printed* at any specific moment, follow the directions in the parentheses for your brand of microcomputer (on the Commodore, press RUN/

> STOP key, on the Apple press both CTRL and C keys, on the TRS-80 press BREAK key—type PRINT X and press the ENTER or RETURN key).

ACTIVITY THREE
PROBLEM SOLVING PROCESS

1. OBJECTIVE:
The students will be able to describe the process used to achieve a given solution.

2. TEACHER PREPARATION:
Provide an opportunity for students to discuss what is meant by reporting on a "process" used to solve a problem.

Use a problem such as guessing a number where each successive guess should bring your students closer to the number that was selected. The problem should involve some logical steps for solution such as you find in a science text, in a puzzle book, or if all else fails, a problem from an arithmetic book.

Emphasize the need to keep track of each step in student thinking by making a careful and complete list of each step on the board.

After students have worked on the problem as a group, give them the following instructions

3. STUDENT INSTRUCTIONS:
After students have worked on the problem as a group, they should write a sentence that expresses the problem, then list the steps they think are involved in its solution.

After exchanging papers, they can check their classmates' papers to see if all the steps needed for a solution are included. Also, they can suggest different solutions. Students should keep these papers because the process they have used will be needed when writing a PILOT or BASIC

> language program in Activity Four at the end of Chapter three.

ACTIVITY FOUR
RUNNING A CAI PROGRAM

1. OBJECTIVE:
The students will be able to run a program and respond to the program material presented.

2. TEACHER PREPARATION:
This is the first of three similar activities. There is a lot of learning and building of self-confidence on the part of students as they interact with a challenge in the form of a CAI program at their level. Examples of the kind of program to select for this activity include the following:

- "Moptown" (Preschool and Primary Grades)—New York: The Learning Company, 1982. Eleven logic games that grow increasingly complex as students are encouraged to develop higher level thinking skills basic to problem solving. Each game builds on skills acquired in the previous game.
- "Vocabulary Skills" (Upper Elementary and Junior High Grades)—Springfield, MA: Milton Bradley, 1982. Students are given the definitions of the three word parts. The meanings of commonly used prefixes, suffixes, and root words are learned by doing matching, true-false, and multiple choice exercises. The program comes with a built-in management system.

Prepare a simple answer page on which students can report the name of the program they used, how they liked it, and what they did not like about it.

3. STUDENT INSTRUCTIONS:
You are to run the program assigned to you, not for a grade, but for the experience of mastering some material

presented by the microcomputer. When you have completed the program, you are to write your ideas and reactions on the answer page given to you so that use of the microcomputer as a learning tool can be improved.

ACTIVITY FIVE

RUNNING A CAI DRILL AND PRACTICE PROGRAM

1. OBJECTIVE:
The student will be able to run a CAI drill and practice program and respond to the program material presented.

2. TEACHER PREPARATION:
This is similar to Activity Four, but the CAI programs suggested are the drill and practice type. Examples of the kind of program to select for this activity include the following:

- "Dueling Digits" (Grades 3-6)—New York: Broderbund Software, 1982. This is an arcade-style game that gives the student drill and practice in forming balanced equations.
- "Spell-N-Time" (Any Grade Spelling)—Fresno: School Courseware Journal, 1980. This is a flash type drill-and-practice program of spelling words chosen by the teacher.

The "Spell-N-Time" program of School Courseware Journal is widely available. You may find your school already has a copy. The program has been translated so that it will run on most brands of microcomputers. The spelling list may be changed daily, weekly, or whenever new spelling words need to be added or the words mastered deleted. Also, the teacher controls the number of words to be presented during each "game." To make those changes follow the directions on pages 3-5 of the *Spell-N-Time* documentation for your brand of microcomputer.

> Prepare a simple answer page on which students can report on the name of the program they used, how they liked it and what they did not like about it.
>
> ### *3. STUDENT INSTRUCTIONS:*
> You are to run the program assigned to you, not for a grade, but for the experience of mastering some material presented by the microcomputer. When you have completed the program, you are to write your ideas and reactions on the answer page given to you so that use of the microcomputer as a learning tool in your school can be improved.

ACTIVITY SIX

RUNNING A CAI SIMULATION PROGRAM

> ### *1. OBJECTIVE:*
> The student will be able to run a CAI simulation program and respond to the program material presented.
>
> ### **2. TEACHER PREPARATION:**
> This is similar to Activity Four and Activity Five, but the CAI programs are of the simulation type. Examples of the kind of program to select for this activity are:
>
> - "Science—Middle School—Volume 3" (Grades 5-8)—St. Paul: Minnesota Educational Computer Consortium, 1980. Five programs are included in this volume that are examples of tutorials and simulations of earth, sea, sky, air, and natural science elements.
> - "Social Studies—Elementary—Volume 3" (or Volume 6) (Grades 2-6)—St. Paul: Minnesota Educational Computer Consortium, 1980. Volume 6 is comprised of social studies simulations. Volume 3 includes two geography drill-and-practice programs in addition to simulation programs.

> Prepare a simple answer page on which students can report on the name of the program they used, how they liked it, and what they did not like about it.
>
> **3. STUDENT INSTRUCTIONS:**
> You are to run the program assigned to you, not for a grade, but for the experience of mastering some material presented by the microcomputer. When you have completed the program, you are to write your ideas and reactions on the answer page given to you so that use of the microcomputer as a learning tool in your school can be evaluated and improved.

NOTES

1. Needle D. Group fights growing use of microcomputers in school. *InfoWorld*. May 10, 1982, pp. 1, 7; See also Committee opposes micros in schools. *Computer Decisions*. June, 1982, p. 22.
2. Skinner B. F. The Technology of Teaching. New York: Appleton-Century-Crofts, 1968, p. 60.
3. The program popularly called Lemonade is actually "Sell Lemonade," part of the Minnesota Educational Computing Consortium diskette No. 704, Elementary Volume 3—Social Studies.
4. The program popularly referred to as Oregon Trail is actually "Oregon," part of the Minnesota Educational Computing Consortium diskette No. 725, Elementary Volume 6—Social Studies.
5. The program popularly referred to as Odell Lake actually has that name and is part of the Minnesota Educational Computing Consortium diskette No. 707, Science Volume 3—Earth/Life Science.
6. For a discussion of the Turtle graphic mode see: Martin K, Bearden D, Muller J H. Turtle graphics on and off the computer. *The Computing Teacher*, November, 1982, pp. 55-58.
7. For a discussion of the Sprite mode see: More about LOGO. *Electronic Education*. January, 1982, p. 14.
8. Buxton M, Taitt H A. Creative programming for young minds. Twentieth Annual AEDS Convention Proceedings. Brittain D,

ed. Washington, DC: The Association for Educational Data Systems, 1982, pp. 240-42.
9. Wager W. Issues in the evaluation of instructional computing programs. *Educational Computer Magazine.* Sept/Oct, 1981, pp. 20-22.
10. Heck W P, Johnson J, Kansky R J. Guidelines for Evaluating Computerized Instructional Materials. Reston, VA: National Council of Teachers of Mathematics, 1981.
11. "Color-Graf" is available from Solectronics, Evanston, IL.
12. "CHROMAtrs" is available from South Shore Computer Concepts, Inc., Hewlett, NY.

3
TEACHER-MADE INSTRUCTIONAL PROGRAMS

There isn't enough time in a teacher's day for routine duties, let alone the added chore of programming instructional lessons made possible by a new technology. Yet time and again we find teachers giving of time that is so scarce, to create a program in BASIC language code that will fit the needs of their students. This is exemplary dedication to the responsibilities of teaching, but is so much more time-demanding than is necessary.

Programming aids are available to any teacher who wants to create instructional or testing programs for microcomputer use by students in a classroom. These take at least two forms, authoring languages and authoring systems, and perhaps a third form, word-processing programs. The advantage of these writing aids for creating instructional programs is that minimal knowledge of any coding or programming language is necessary. In almost every computer programming language, you find the substitution of letters, numbers, or symbols arranged in accordance with the rules of the computer language rather than according to the English sentences you are used to using. In some computer languages, short words are used that have special meanings that are similar to the usual English meaning. In other computer languages, such as PILOT, only eight single-letter core statements need to be learned in order to produce a computer program. In contrast, BASIC as a programming language requires 16 multiletter statements to achieve the same result. The box below lists the PILOT core statements and the BASIC programming statements that are applicable to at least one brand of microcomputer. The use of these PILOT statements is described later in this chapter. The uses of the BASIC programming statements can be found in any of several books on BASIC listed in the Recommended Readings and Media section.

PILOT CORE STATEMENTS

T—type, A—accept, M—match, J—jump, E—end, U—use, C—compute, and R—remark.

BASIC PROGRAMMING STATEMENTS

READ, DATA, PRINT, LET, GOTO, IF—THEN, FOR—NEXT, END, INPUT, DEF, GOSUB, RETURN, RESTORE, REM, DIM, STOP.

Authoring systems and word-processing programs have a common requirement. This requirement is for the teacher to decide on the format of the text, such as margins, spacing, and centering. Although rules must be followed when using an authoring system or a word-processing program, they seem less demanding to many teachers than the rules identified with BASIC or another programming language. Teachers often find similarities in the instructional creativity required when using a computer with an authoring system or a word-processing program and using a typewriter to create an instructional lesson.

In this chapter you will learn about:
- PILOT as an authoring aid
- Authoring systems for CAI programs
- Word processing programs for student reading and writing activity
- Word processing programs for teacher-generated print materials for classroom use

Each topic is expanded by (1) the reasons for instructional classroom use, (2) a list of Recommended Readings and Media for further learning, and (3) learning activities for students.

PILOT AS AN AUTHORING AID

One of the earliest efforts to create a programming language that is easy to learn and use was the 1970 creation of PILOT by Dr. John Starkweather of the University of California Medical Center at San Francisco.[1] The acronym stands for Programmed Inquiry Learning Or Teaching. The eight core statements used in PILOT can be divided into the input and output statements, the control statements, and the special purpose statements.

The input and output statements are:

- T stands for type or text. It can be a tutorial input.
- A stands for accept or answer.
- M stands for match. Does the answer correspond to the answer that is expected or sought?

These letters can be used without any other letters to create a limited program of instruction. However, a PILOT program disk is needed in order to use PILOT as an authoring language. Note that in the example below, two modifying letters were added to the T statement, specifically Y and N, representing "text if yes" and "text if no" in response to the M statement.

The input and output statements, although useful in a limited way, often need a control statement such as listed below:

> J stands for jump. The jump can be forward or backward in the program and is controlled by inserting an asterisk (*) and a label in front of the statement line where the program is to operate next.

EXAMPLE

T: HI! IS THIS YOUR FIRST EXPERIENCE ON
T: A MICROCOMPUTER?

A:
M: YES/YEAH/SURE
TY: I HOPE YOU ENJOY YOUR EXPERIENCE
TN: WELL, I HOPE THIS TIME IS AS GOOD AN
TN: EXPERIENCE AS THE LAST TIME.
T: IN THE AREA OF EDUCATIONAL USE OF
T: MICROCOMPUTERS, WHAT ARE YOUR
T: MAIN INTERESTS?
A:

U stands for use. It has the same idea as *jump*, but in the language of computer operations is considered a subroutine that will carry out some limited programming purpose and then return to the line that followed the U statement when it encounters E.

E stands for end. It may be the very end of the program, or it may represent the end of the U subroutine.

If you add these three control statements to the earlier three input and output statements, a more useful instructional program can be created. Now you are ready to consider the last of the core statements used in programming in PILOT.

EXAMPLE

R: Lesson 17, pages 34-35
T: MONDAY'S MONEY EQUALS?
A: #M
T: TUESDAY'S MONEY EQUALS?
A: #T
C: #D = #M — #T
T: HOW MUCH IS LEFT TO SPEND ON

T: WEDNESDAY? D#

E:

These are the special-purpose statements:

R stands for remark. It is useful to you as a teacher to enter remarks that will not be shown on the screen as part of the program, but that serve to remind you of your intentions in creating the program.

C stands for compute. It causes the computer to calculate the formula as set forth on the line that follows the C command. PILOT uses +, −, /, and * as the symbols for addition, subtraction, division, and multiplication, respectively. The upward arrow is used as the signal for calculating the power indicated, an upward arrow 2 would signal the computer to square a number.

As you examine various versions of PILOT you will undoubtedly find some things that differ from the eight statements described above. Many of the commercial PILOT programs provide graphics as well as sound commands, and some provide for color selection. However, no matter what differences are encountered, the fundamental ideas are the same. The real test of the usefulness of PILOT as a tool for teacher use in creating instructional materials for students is whether it can easily become part of your teaching repertoire. Many teachers have reported that PILOT is easily learned in a very short time. A number of fifth and sixth grade teachers have used PILOT as a means of teaching their students to begin programming. PILOT is used in many junior high school classrooms as an introduction to programming microcomputers.

AUTHORING SYSTEMS FOR CAI PROGRAMS

The use of PILOT requires a minimal amount of programming skill, but the use of an authoring system requires no programming skill whatsoever. Fundamentally, a lesson created by the teacher and typed on the microcomputer keyboard can be translated by an authoring system into the necessary machine language code that a microcomputer can understand and act on. You can think of the microcomputer authoring system as performing your programming coding tasks for you. There is an authoring system available for almost every brand of microcomputer. You are encouraged to consult the Material Resources in the Appendix for names, addresses, and microcomputer requirements and then ask for a demonstration or preview before purchase.

You may ask, "What is so special about authoring systems? Why should I be interested?" The answer lies in the comparative time requirements of using BASIC, PILOT, and an authoring system to create an instructional lesson. A BASIC program typically requires approximately 200 hours of programming to create a lesson useful in classroom instruction, although this varies with the type of lesson involved. In contrast, using either PILOT or an authoring system will require approximately 15 hours of work at the microcomputer keyboard to create a comparable lesson. Now, the reason many teachers prefer an authoring system over PILOT is that competence in using PILOT will take two weeks or longer to develop, while competence in using an authoring system can be gained in one to three days. PILOT offers almost no word processing and very limited classroom management record keeping, whereas authoring systems provide varying capabilities in both of these areas.

Before you become too enthused about obtaining and using an authoring system, it would be prudent to explore just what is expected of you, as a teacher, in creating any microcomputer instructional program. After all, using an authoring system to create CAI is part of the programmed instruction tradition. There are innumerable guides to undertaking the writing of programmed instruction. Many of these programmed instruction guides do not take into account the capabilities of the microcomputer and limit their focus to the capabilities of print media. Important elements to consider in creating an effective CAI program are that the program be:

- Learner controlled
- Adaptive and responsive to individualization
- Modular and structured in hierarchical form

CAI can be fun!

In addition to these requirements,

- The skill mastery expected must agree with originally stated performance objectives
- Progress should be measured and recorded
- Diagnostic and prescriptive strategies should be used
- Programs should reflect multisensory formats where justified by program content and microcomputer capability; color, sound, and graphics should never be used simply to show off the author's skill or the microcomputer's capability

You may already be aware of CAI programs such as the "PLATO" series of Control Data Corporation. Although among the best known today, it was not the first effort in this direction. Authoring systems that preceded "PLATO" were such programs as "TIP," an acronym for Translator of Interactive Programs, and "COURSEWRITER." Other CAI authoring systems you may have read about include "Ticcit" from Brigham Young University, "Tutor," and "Planit." The most frequent forms of CAI are tutorial, drill-and-practice, problem-solving, and simulation programs.

An ample supply of ideas are to be found in the literature of instructional technology that you may find useful in planning and creating a CAI lesson for your students using an authoring system. A "storyboard" is a visual planning technique widely used in movie-making, animated cartoons, and TV production; it is an aid to good CAI lesson planning. For example, think of a lesson you have introduced to your students in the past week and imagine that you are a human form of a microcomputer located in the classroom and responding to pupils' recitation. Using information from that scenario, discover for yourself just how much of the CAI checksheet on the following page you can fill in. Use the following ten steps as a guide in creating some ideas that could be translated into a microcomputer CAI program when you have access to an authoring system. There are decisions that need to be made about:

1. An area of instruction
2. A desired learning outcome
3. The specific content involved in the desired learning outcome
4. The instructional activities to be used
5. The sequencing of material
6. The evaluation tactic
7. The answer matching options
8. The screen display features
9. The appropriate time limits for student study, student response, and the time records to be kept
10. Other records to keep

A storyboard is no more difficult to create than to thumbtack 3 × 5 cards to a bulletin board where each card represents a rough sketch of a "learning scene" that you want to create on the microcomputer screen. The cards can be moved easily and, thus, the sequence of learning screens can be modified before using an authoring system to create the final CAI on your brand of microcomputer. One of the most useful aspects of an authoring system is the ease with which you as the teacher and author can create text or graphics and swing from one form to another as your storyboard plan dictates. You need not create all of the text screens before forming the graphic screens, nor vice versa. Moreover, you can revise your earlier screens of material and even add more screens after you have completed your CAI lesson, as you see the need to do so.

Making a storyboard.

One of the interesting by-products of using either PILOT or an authoring system to create a student CAI lesson is that teachers report learning more about their own teaching styles in the process. This is undoubtedly the product of the greater attention to detail that teachers find themselves involved with when creating a CAI lesson. The checksheet is not intended to provide all of the elements that may be appropriate and needed in using an authoring system to create CAI. For example, your instructional lesson may call for specifically recognizing previously learned concepts needed as a prerequisite to undertaking the lesson. If the authoring system you are using provides for random selection of responses to correct and incorrect answers from a teacher-provided pool of such answers, you will need to give yourself some reminder of that requirement. Moreover, if your authoring system provides for both backward and forward branching, you will need to give yourself a reminder space on such a checksheet. The reminder will indicate your criteria for advancement to another lesson, as well as your criteria for a return to a more elementary lesson. Finally, you may want to add a checksheet provision about the amount of time permitted for answers and whether you want those time intervals recorded along with the achievement or lack of achievement of your students.

CAI CHECKSHEET

Lesson Topic   Lesson Title

_____   _____

_____   _____

Lesson Objective

_____

_____

Narrative or Tutorial Text

_____

_____

Question

_____

_____

Trials Allowed   Answer Form

_____   _____

_____   _____

Expected Answer	Second Possible Answer	Third Possible Answer
_____	_____	_____
_____	_____	_____
_____	_____	_____

Reply for Correct Answer

_____

_____

Reply for Other Answers

_____

_____

Reply for Last Attempt Allowed

_____

_____

If Hint/Help Request Permitted: Reply?

_____

_____

Before purchasing an authoring system, you may want to set down some of the qualities to consider. With the breadth of choices available, it seems unwise to settle for less than the following:

- Flexible answer options within questions

- Flexible branching both forward and backward
- Answer-matching capabilities that include word matches (partial spelling matches preferable), single letter, number, symbol, or cursor movement entry matches
- Record-keeping capability on response times
- Individual student scores, summary and group records by question capabilities
- Ability to use graphics, upper and lower case letters, and screen formatting, if not automatic formatting (color and sound capabilities may be a plus depending on subject and grade level)
- Ease of use by a teacher

You can expect:

- 48K of memory to be required
- Two disk drives will be required for creating lessons
- Only one drive required to use the lesson
- Authoring programs to cost between $70 and $300, although price does not appear to indicate quality or usefulness

Moreover, you should be aware that some authoring system disks cannot be copied, even for archival purposes.

The development of commercial versions of PILOT and of authoring systems has provided teachers with alternatives to programming instructional materials in BASIC. Teachers who have used either PILOT or an authoring system report that they learn the use of either approach at a faster rate the more they use it. First, with increased microcomputer familiarity, the productivity of the teacher using PILOT or an authoring system is significantly improved. Second, teachers experienced increased ease in creating CAI or programmed lesson material. Third, increased speed and accuracy in using either an authoring system or PILOT is experienced as a teacher engages in creating additional instructional materials with either approach.

WORD-PROCESSING PROGRAMS FOR STUDENT READING AND WRITING

Imagine the excitement of your students as they discover the control they can exercise over the microcomputer when, with a word-processing program in the microcomputer's memory, the student begins to use the keyboard as a typewriter. Primary school children are delighted with seeing their names or some other message on the screen as a result of their pressing letters on the keyboard. Upper elementary school children respond with enthusiasm to the ease in changing the spelling of a word, to the ease of moving a word or a sentence to another location. Teachers who offer their students the experience of seeing their input to the microcomputer screen become a printed reality on a classroom printer report high levels of pride and pleasure on the part of the student. Their work is now printed on real paper in type form like that they read in their textbooks. For those teachers who have not become familiar with the uses of microcomputers in creating student reading and writing materials, there are a number of reports and articles you will find listed in the Recommended Readings and Media section that describe classroom successes in using word processing. Included are descriptions of microcomputer use in such word-processing activities as

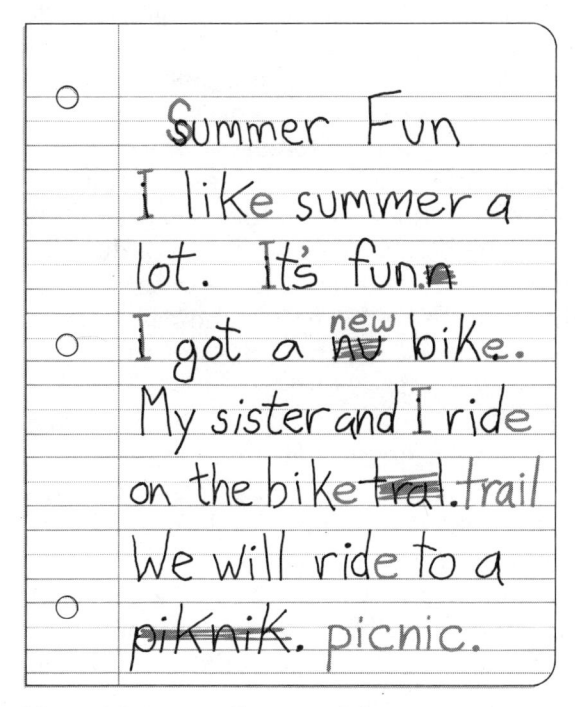

> Summer Fun
> I like summer a lot. It's fun.
> I got a new bike.
> My sister and I ride on the bike trail.
> We will ride to a picnic.

Rewriting without pencil-cramped fingers or sweaty palms.

preschool children writing eight-line stories, primary children creating language experience stories, a child with learning difficulties creating a two-line letter, as well as references to such reading and writing activities as sentence expansion, sentence reorganization, sentence combination, writing poetry, and writing a creative story.

The magic of word processing for students probably stems from three elements: (1) use of new technology; (2) use of the write-correct-rewrite approach is more palatable because corrections are more easily made when there is no pencil to hold in a special way by fingers that are cramped and sweaty; and (3) the process of composing is faster. Teachers who have observed children composing letters, stories, poems, and reports are surprised at the lack of dawdling they have come to expect from some of their students. Ideas seem to flow faster and become a text image on the screen more rapidly with a microcomputer than with pencil and paper. Children dislike working with a messy page. They often crumple up a page on which they have made what they regard as a mistake and then painstakingly rewrite the few words they had written before. This is just not part of the microcomputer word-processing experience. Mistakes are easy to correct, as even the young student discovers.

You may be among those teachers who are asking what microcomputer word processing is all about. It is a system that permits typing any kind of alphabetic text material on a microcomputer keyboard, seeing the text displayed on the screen of the monitor, and being able to make corrections in spelling, punctuation, and word choices with a few key strokes. The commands involved are not difficult to learn.

At a recent conference, a number of teachers engaged in a lively exchange of views on the easiest word-processing program to use with students. The teachers present objected to the necessity of using a double ESCAPE keystroke in order to move the cursor up, down, right, or left. Even with a word-processing system as relatively simple for children to use as the "Scripsit"[2] program, the command structures are more complex than necessary. "The Bank Street Writer"[3] is a word-processing program created especially for classroom use. As the student creates the written material on the keyboard, the text appears inside a bordered area that covers most of the screen. Above the bordered area is a fixed display of commands and prompts that remind the student of how to make corrections (erase, replace, and move text). Some other word-processing programs assist the user by providing information on the commands to use for text corrections when the user types H for help or the full word, "Help."

Most teachers think children should see letters in both upper and lower case with true descenders (the tail of those letters that extend below the line such as g, j, p, q, and y) on the screen as well as on the printed page. If this is your view, don't settle for a microcomputer, word-processing program, or printer that gives you less than you expect. Teachers using either the Atari or Apple brands of microcomputers should consider using "The Bank Street Writer," which gives upper and lower case letters on the screen and will generate upper and lower case letters on printers that have that print capacity. Almost every brand of microcomputer can be equipped to provide word processing that provides upper and lower case with either a software program or a hardware modification.

To gain an understanding of how corrections are made when using a word-processing program, two fundamental instructions (deleting and inserting) are given in the section that follows.

Assume that you have one or more students who have created a two-line story using the "Scripsit" program on a TRS-80 microcomputer or using "The Bank Street Writer" on an Apple. Note that the written text of each child appears on the screen in upper and lower case letters. If one of your students realizes that an incorrect letter has been typed on the TRS-80 using "Scripsit," the leftward arrow key is used to backspace and then the student retypes the correct letter. In "The Bank Street Writer," each backspace stroke erases the letter or number on the screen. When using the backspace with "Scripsit," no erasure takes place. In both programs, the letter to be corrected is simply overtyped. There is no erasing, no mess, and no torn paper. The microcomputer immediately substitutes the new letter for the old letter. Two further examples are provided below to illustrate how useful a word-processing program can be. Just remember it takes more words to describe the process than you or your students will find it takes to accomplish the task.

SCRIPSIT EXAMPLE

TO DELETE ONE WORD:
Place the cursor _ on the first letter
Hold down @
Press D and release
Press Z and release—and now release @

TO DELETE ONE SENTENCE:
Place the cursor _ on the first letter
Hold down @
Press D and release
Press X and release—and now release @

TO INSERT A WORD, PHRASE, OR SENTENCE:
Place the cursor _ where you want the insert
Hold down @
Press S and release
Press X and release
Type in the word, phrase, or sentence
Then press CLEAR

Teachers at all grade levels report that students tend to write more when using a microcomputer word-processing program than they do when using pencil and paper. The microcomputer eliminates the motor and dexterity problems some children experience when attempting to write with a pencil. Another reason students tend to write more may be that corrections are easily made when using a word-processing program.

BANK STREET WRITER EXAMPLE

TO DELETE ONE WORD, ONE SENTENCE or MORE:
Press ESCape key to move from Write menu to Edit menu.

Use the Left or Right arrow to move the highlighted cursor at the top of the screen to ERASE and press RETURN key. Follow the instruction at the top of the screen to "PLACE CURSOR AT BEGINNING OF TEXT TO ERASE THEN PRESS RETURN." The cursor is moved on the text screen by using the J key to move leftward, the K key to move to the right, the I key to move upward, and the M key to move down. Upon pressing RETURN, your student sees an instruction at the top of the screen that reads, "PLACE CURSOR AT END OF TEXT TO ERASE THEN PRESS RETURN." As the K key is pressed to move the cursor to the right, the word or sentence that is to be erased is highlighted. When RETURN is pressed, the instruction message at the top of the screen reads, "ARE YOU SURE YOU WANT TO ERASE HIGHLIGHTED TEXT (Y/N)?" The student types Y and the material that had been marked for deletion is gone. Pressing the ESCape key returns the student to the Write menu and the ability to write further text.

TO INSERT A WORD, PHRASE, OR SENTENCE:
Press ESCape key to move from Write menu to Edit menu. The student needs to move the cursor so that it is positioned on the text screen where the insertion is desired. The cursor is moved on the text screen by using the J key to move leftward, the K key to move to the right, the I key to move upward, and the M key to move down. When the cursor is in the desired position, press ESCape key to return to the Write menu and begin typing the insertion. The text to the right of where the insertion is being made will be moved out of the way by each keystroke, including strokes of the space bar. When the insertion has been completed, the ESCape key must be pressed again to gain access to the Edit menu and to move the cursor from the end of the insertion to the next place where further new text is to be typed. The ESCape key is then pressed again to return to the Write menu and the user is able to resume creation of new text.

Teachers and students who have used word-processing programs with microcomputers do not report any limitation on creativity. Perhaps the ease in composing and in revising text material contributes to even more creativity than is experienced with pencil-and-paper approaches. However, there are drawbacks to student use of word processing. It is clearly more expensive than pencil and paper and does require a relatively fixed location. Although microcomputers are portable, they are certainly not as portable as a pencil and paper. Some teachers express concern that word processing can only be effective with students who have learned touch typing. Some elementary teachers fear that children who learn to type will not want to master handwriting. Touch typing is not a requirement for effective use of a word-processing program on a microcomputer, although familiarity with the keyboard is desirable. Touch typing, in the traditional sense, may be a hindrance to using a word-processing program on a microcomputer because some keyboards are very sensitive and may not tolerate even the light touch of fingers resting on the "home" keys. What is useful, and achievable, even with primary-grade children is teaching the location of the keys. There are several microcomputer programs listed in the Recommended Readings and Media section that are worth considering. These programs provide even a young child with practice in finding the location of keys on the microcomputer keyboard. In addition, there are practice keyboards, such as the Computer Practice Keyboard Company product,[4] that teach familiarity with specific microcomputer keyboards.

In spite of these drawbacks, a word-processing program can be used in many ways to enhance the reading-and-writing learning process and the list keeps growing as creative teachers use microcomputers in language arts teaching.

WORD-PROCESSING PROGRAMS FOR TEACHER-GENERATED PRINT MATERIALS

The needs of teachers and school administrative personnel for a word-processing system are quite different from the needs of students. The advent of word processing may be the most significant tool for teacher use in decades. This is because word-processing programs make possible saving all kinds of written materials on cassette tape or disk for later revision and use. No longer does a stencil or ditto master have to be saved with care in the hope that it can be used with another class or put through a copying machine to make a new ditto master. It does not matter whether the word-processing text saved is a quiz, an end of the unit test, a handout on the use of verbs, or a notice of the class party. The text that has been saved can be retrieved by its file name and the changes can be made for a new group of students. The revised version is then ready for printing. In one school where teachers make heavy use of microcomputer word processing, each teacher creates a notebook in which one printed copy of each quiz, test, or handout is placed. At the top of each page is the file name under which the printed copy has been saved and the name or number of the diskette.

The Materials Resource list gives the name and microcomputer requirements for each of the most popular word-processing programs. You will also find details on specialized programs that can be used with word-processing programs. These specialized programs take two forms. The first is the electronic dictionary that checks the spelling of every word in the word-processing text you have created. Imagine writing a report on the classroom piloting of a new textbook or microcomputer program for the superintendent of your district. If you have no spelling mistakes, within 15 seconds of the time you subject your prose to checking by the microcomputer dictionary program, you will know your report is free of spelling mistakes. If there are errors, or if there are words not at that point recorded in the dictionary memory, the program will pause with the cursor flashing at the beginning of the misspelled word or of the word that is not in memory and patiently wait for you to decide if the word is spelled wrong, or whether it is a new word you want listed in the dictionary memory for future use. The second specialized word processing program is a prose editor. The most widely known is "Grammatik,"[5] which is available for CP/M, TRS-80, and IBM-PC brands of microcomputers. This program is similar to having an English teacher at your side as you write. The error codes that this program uses are listed below.

A—archaic usage
B—unbalanced " " or ( )
C—capitalization error
D—doubled word or punctuation (*now now* or *!!*)
E—user-defined error (this provides for user input of specific errors you know you tend to make in your writing)
G—gender-specific term
I—informal usage (*ain't*)
J—jargon or technical term
K—awkward usage (*and/or*)
M—commonly misused word
O—overworked or trite wording
P—punctuation error
R—redundant phrase (*seldom ever*)
S—spelling error
T—trademark (*Xerox* is not a verb)
U—improper usage
V—vague adverb
W—wordy phrase

"Grammatik" does not check for subject–verb agreement, does not know the meaning of words, and cannot check for split infinitives or dangling participles. "Grammatik" contains a dictionary of 500 commonly misused phrases. After "Grammatik" has analyzed a word-processing text, it provides a summary of the number of sentences and the number of words. A report on the average sentence length in number of words and the average word length in number of letters is also given. The number of imperatives and the number of questions in the text are reported, as are the number of sentences of 14 words or less and the number of sentences with 30 words or more. Also reported are the number of prepositions used and the number of times "to be's" have been used. The "Grammatik" program reads what has been written in a word-processing text with more care than even the most dedicated English teacher. When a problem is found, the program stops reading and waits for your decision on change, deletion, or no change, and proceeds with its checking only after you hit ENTER or an equivalent key on your microcomputer.

When using a word-processing program, almost any teacher or educational administrator is faced with the need to underline and to insert superscripts to indicate a footnote. Word-processing programs that are appropriate for such formal writing are indicated as providing that capability in the Material Resources list. The greatest problem is acquiring a letter quality printer that will successfully interface with the microcomputer and the word-processing program selected. If you face the need to do formal writing using word processing, insist that the computer store physically prove that the printer, microcomputer, and the chosen word-processing program work together before any purchase decision is made.

SUMMARY

This chapter introduced several programming aids to the teacher who wants to develop instructional programs for the microcomputer. Each reader will find different values in the four sections of the chapter. Only the teacher can determine what is best suited for the teaching and learning style in that classroom. Programming aids such as PILOT or an authoring system can facilitate the teacher's use of the microcomputer as a powerful teaching tool.

An authoring system is certainly a time-saver when compared to writing all the lines of BASIC code that a CAI program requires. Moreover, the availability of significant computer managed instruction (CMI) elements in the better authoring systems is a definite advantage. In evaluating software for classroom use, you will be wise to look for the record-keeping ability in a program that represents a minimum CMI capability. Because this kind of record-keeping ability is found in authoring systems you might use for yourself in creating a microcomputer lesson for your students, it seems only good sense to look for that same ability in the prepared programs you are considering. Moreover, the ability of authoring systems to provide the teacher with both individual student records and a class summary record on problems encountered is helpful not only in record keeping, but also in planning instruction.

Teachers of language arts and social studies subjects may have more enthusiasm for the student word-processing section than teachers of science and mathematics. However, in the elementary school grades as well as in secondary school grades, creating opportunities for student writing is a high priority. Evidence suggests that the classroom usefulness of a word-processing program reflects the attitude of the teacher about the importance of writing practice and the attitude of the teacher about using the microcomputer.

Finally, every teacher will find some usefulness in the word-processing capability of the microcomputer when creating tests and classroom learning materials. Those teachers and educational administrators who are involved in graduate study can find the appropriate word-processing program a very useful aid in completing the kinds of formal writing often required in advanced study.

ACTIVITY ONE

SIMPLE PROGRAMMING IN PILOT

1. OBJECTIVE:
The student will be able to program a dialogue in the PILOT language.

2. TEACHER PREPARATION:
Refer to PILOT AS AN AUTHORING AID section of Chapter three. You will note that the first example ends with accepting the answer to the question: "In the area of educational use of microcomputers, what are your main interests?" This example could be extended with further lines of code that would complete the thought involved.

T: YOU MAY ALREADY KNOW THAT COMPUTER-ASSISTED INSTRUCTION IS AN IMPORTANT EDUCATIONAL USE OF MICROCOMPUTERS.

T: HAVE YOU EVER USED A COMPUTER-ASSISTED INSTRUCTIONAL PROGRAM?

A:

TN: I WOULD URGE YOU TO TRY IT!

J: *X

TY: DID YOU LIKE THE EXPERIENCE?

M: YES/YEAH/SURE

TY: I DID TOO! WELL, SEE YOU LATER.

*X:

E:

You will need to present the ideas involved in PILOT programming to your students. With the PILOT language loaded in your microcomputer, type in the example given above. You should note that the example uses a colon following the single letter command. Your version of PILOT may use a semicolon, a single quotation mark, or some other delimiter. Simply substitute the symbol you must use for the colon used in the example. You would be wise not to use the letter commands, J and U, nor any graphics, color, or sound commands until you and your students have achieved success with the more fundamental T, A, M, R, and C command letters. After students have written their versions on lined paper, have them compare what they have completed with a partner you assign. Then give them time on a microcomputer to type in their program.

3. STUDENT INSTRUCTIONS:
Use the beginning program in PILOT you have been given as the basis for adding your own ideas. You are to complete the PILOT program in a handwritten version and compare what you have written with the partner you have been assigned. Then if you both think the program will run, type in your program on the microcomputer keyboard, type RUN, and respond to the inputs as required by the program.

ACTIVITY TWO

ADDITIONAL PROGRAMMING IN PILOT

1. OBJECTIVE:
The student will be able to program calculations in the PILOT language.

2. TEACHER PREPARATION:
Refer to PILOT AS AN AUTHORING AID section of Chapter three. You will note that the second example ends with the calculation of what is left to spend on Wednesday. This example could be extended with further lines of code that would complete the week's expenditure of money and the calculations involved.

3. STUDENT INSTRUCTIONS:
Use the beginning program in PILOT you have been given as the basis for adding your own ideas on further calculations. You are to complete the PILOT program in a handwritten version. Compare what you have written with the program of the partner you have been assigned. Then, if you both think the program will run, type in your program on the microcomputer keyboard, type RUN, and respond to the inputs as required by the program.

ACTIVITY THREE

WORD PROCESSING

1. OBJECTIVE:
The student will be able to replace specific words in a teacher-prepared paragraph with synonyms using a word-processing program.

2. TEACHER PREPARATION:
Using a word-processing program, create a paragraph in

which you use capital letters to indicate the words you want the student to replace with a synonym. Your instructions to students on the microcomputer screen might read as follows:

3. STUDENT INSTRUCTIONS:
Read the paragraph below. Erase each of the capitalized words. Type in another word in place of each erased word that has the same meaning and makes sense in the sentence. Save your corrected paragraph under your own name on the utility disk provided.

ACTIVITY FOUR

CONVERTING PROBLEM-SOLVING PROCESS TO PROGRAMMING SOLUTION

1. OBJECTIVE:
The student will be able to write a program in PILOT or BASIC programming code to solve the problem with the process used in Activity Three of Chapter two.

2. TEACHER PREPARATION:
Before students can undertake this activity, they must be introduced to programming in PILOT or BASIC. The background on the PILOT language in Chapter three should be sufficient to permit students to convert their written statements in the solution process they created in Activity Three of Chapter two into a successful PILOT program. One drawback to using PILOT is that it requires a disk program that contains the PILOT language. Every microcomputer has BASIC available as a language, even in microcomputers that do not have disk-drive capabilities. Thus the choice of whether to use PILOT or BASIC as a language with students is up to you. Teachers report a better result if all the students in a class use either PILOT or BASIC at a given time.

3. STUDENT INSTRUCTIONS:
You are to work in pairs to convert the written problem solution into a PILOT (or BASIC) program. Write out your program in detail. Pretend you are a computer and talk your way through the lines of code you write. When you think it is ready to RUN, get time on the microcomputer, key in your program, carefully proofread each line as it appears on the screen against the handwritten version. Then type RUN, and press ENTER or RETURN.

ACTIVITY FIVE

ADDITIONAL WORD PROCESSING

1. OBJECTIVE:
The student will become aware of the variety of ways classmates will develop a common beginning into quite different narratives.

2. TEACHER PREPARATION:
Create a three-line beginning to a story that is appropriate to the age and life experience of your student group. For example:
   Bob and Tom sat on a log beside the lake.
   It was a warm day. They had hiked three miles since lunch. Now they were tired.
Your *** Teacher
Type a row of name and asterisks, as shown above, then instruct your students to write not more than four additional lines to add to the story beginning. Each student should then use the space bar or other key appropriate to your word-processing program to move the story up the screen until only the last sentence (or line or two) are showing. Have each student type a row of name and asterisks like the example given below, using his or her first name and last name.

Student *************************************** Name
When all of your students have had a turn, then return to the top of the screen and slowly scroll down the screen asking each student to read his or her contribution in turn.

Before you try to compose the instructions for your students using a word-processing program, try your hand at writing a sample story starter. Once you have created a story using a word-processing program, be sure to save it with a file name if you want to read it at a later time and check for improvement of your student's writing later in the school year.

3. STUDENT INSTRUCTIONS:

You are to write not more than four additional lines to the beginning of the story (only the last two lines are displayed). Then type a line of asterisks and your name, like the example on the screen above. You are to move your writing that appears on the screen up so that only the last two lines of your story can be seen by the next student.

ACTIVITY SIX

PROGRAMMING A WORD PROBLEM USING PILOT

1. STUDENT OBJECTIVE:

The student will be able to write a program for solving a word problem in the PILOT language.

2. TEACHER PREPARATION:

This activity builds on student experiences in Activity One above. You will need to remind students of the rules of PILOT commands, T, A, M, R, and C. A story problem from the student's arithmetic book may be used to assign the solving of the problem by writing a program in the PILOT language. Alternatively, you may want the students to create a PILOT program that provides practice in solving this type of problem. It is desirable to have students write their program on paper first. Then have them compare their work with an assigned partner before time is given on the microcomputer to type in their program and RUN it.

3. STUDENT INSTRUCTIONS:
Use the word problem example you have been given as the basis for writing a program in the PILOT language to solve the problem. You are to complete the PILOT program in a handwritten version first. Compare what you have written with the partner you have been assigned. Then if you both think the program will run, type in your program on the microcomputer keyboard, type RUN, and respond to the input cues as required by the program. If the program will not RUN or does not solve the problem, check to make sure each line of PILOT code was correctly typed on the microcomputer keyboard.

ACTIVITY SEVEN

PROGRAMMING A WORD PROBLEM USING BASIC

1. STUDENT OBJECTIVE:
The student will be able to write a program to solve a word problem in the BASIC language.

2. TEACHER PREPARATION:
This activity builds on student experiences in Activities Five and Seven in Chapter one. You will need to remind students about the rules in BASIC on PRINT and INPUT, and about the difference between variables like A$ and A. You will need to find a story problem in the student's arithmetic book (probably one they have already solved) and assign the writing of a BASIC program to solve the problem. It is desirable to have students write their program on paper first. Then have them compare their work with an assigned partner before they are given time

on the microcomputer to type in their program and RUN it.

3. STUDENT INSTRUCTIONS:
Use the word problem example given to you as the basis for writing a program in the BASIC language for solving the problem. You are to complete the BASIC program in a handwritten version first. Compare what you have written with the partner you have been assigned. Then if you both think the program will run, type in your program on the microcomputer keyboard, type RUN, and respond to the input cues as required by the program. If the program will not RUN or does not solve the problem, check to make sure each line of BASIC code was correctly typed on the microcomputer keyboard.

ACTIVITY EIGHT
USING THE PILOT J COMMAND

1. OBJECTIVE:
The student will be able to change or add to a previously written PILOT program by using the PILOT J command.

2. TEACHER PREPARATION:
You will need to study and experiment with the example below. You should enter this short PILOT program on your microcomputer. Be certain that you use the delimiter (colon, semicolon, etc.) your system requires. Make sure that the example you write on the board for student guidance will RUN.

    T: JOHN HAS THE MEASLES

    J: *Q

    T: THIS LINE WILL NEVER BE SEEN

    T: NOR WILL YOU GET THE MEASLES

> *Q:
>   T: HIS BASEBALL TEAM LOST THE GAME.
>
> While the example above provides for a jump to a later T statement, the jump could have been back to an earlier T statement. The J(ump) command works in both directions. You can have more than a single jump (your PILOT program will have some predetermined limit on how many), but each jump must use a different character, *Q can only be used once in a program, but *X could be used, as could *Y, and so forth.
>
> Experience suggests the desirability of having students use a PILOT program they have already written and demonstrated will run. Then have them write out their addition of the J command to this previous program on paper. Then have them compare their work with an assigned partner, before they have time on the microcomputer to type in their program and RUN it.
>
> **3. STUDENT INSTRUCTIONS:**
> Use a previous program you have written and RUN in the PILOT language as the basis for adding the use of the J command. You are to complete the new PILOT program in a handwritten version first. Compare what you have written with the partner you have been assigned. Then if you both think the program will run, type in your program on the microcomputer keyboard, type RUN, and respond as required by the program. If the program will not RUN or does not solve the problem, check to make sure each line of PILOT code was correctly typed on the microcomputer keyboard.

ACTIVITY NINE

CONVERTING BETWEEN PILOT AND BASIC

> **1. OBJECTIVE:**
> The student will be able to convert a program written in the PILOT language to the BASIC language or vice versa.

2. TEACHER PREPARATION:

If you have used both PILOT and BASIC in the activities provided in this chapter and in Chapter one (Chapter one: Activities Five, Six, and Seven; Chapter three: Activities One, Two, Four, Six, Seven, and Eight), you will need to remind students of the different rules that apply. Students should use a program in PILOT or in BASIC they have previously written and successfully RUN. Assigning each student a partner with whom they are to review their written program before they type it on the microcomputer keyboard will be helpful.

3. STUDENT INSTRUCTIONS:

Use a previous program you have written and RUN in PILOT or in BASIC as the basis for converting that program to the other language. Complete the new program in a handwritten version first. Compare what you have written with the partner you have been assigned. Then, if you both think the program will run, type in your program on the microcomputer keyboard, type RUN, and respond to the inputs as required by the program. If the program will not RUN or does not solve the problem, check to make sure each line of PILOT code or BASIC code was correctly typed on the microcomputer keyboard.

NOTES

1. For a discussion of the work of Dr. John Starkweather and his approach in creating PILOT see: Yob G. PILOT. *Creative Computing.* May/June, 1977, p. 57.
2. "Scripsit" is available from Radio Shack Division, Tandy Corporation, Fort Worth, Texas.
3. "Bank Street Writer" is available from Broderbund Software, San Rafael, California, or Scholastic, Inc., New York.
4. "Computer keyboard" is available from Computer Practice Keyboard Company, Union City, New Jersey.
5. "Grammatik" is available from Aspen Software, Tijeras, New Mexico.

4
IMPLICATIONS OF CAI AND CMI

Each new tool employed in teaching encounters a similar regimen of testing to see whether it can be used with confidence, that it does confer some measurable benefit, and that it does not create new problems in the teaching and learning experience. In the case of microcomputers, the earlier work involving computer-assisted learning has shortened the validation period, at least for those who are willing to accept the notion that a microcomputer is simply a much smaller version of the large computer on which most of the educational research was focused.

WHAT DOES RESEARCH SUGGEST ABOUT EXPECTATIONS?

Each of the studies referred to in the following paragraphs is identified in the footnotes at the end of this chapter. The eight elementary school studies of CAI effectiveness, as well as the three junior high school and the three high school studies are a reasonable sampling of the available serious research that has been done on consequences of using CAI in a variety of educational settings. The subject areas involved in these studies included mathematics, reading, language arts, social studies, science, and business education. Every grade level from kindergarten through high school is represented in one or more of the studies described below.

ELEMENTARY SCHOOL STUDIES

Suppes and Morningstar[1] undertook the study of selected research sites located in California and Mississippi where CAI drill and practice were used to supplement mathematics instruction for grades one through six. In California and Mississippi, they found significantly higher mathematics scores for the CAI group of students than for the control group. Harris[2] reported that students using CAI in third grade and sixth grade mathematics scored significantly higher than nonCAI students. On the other hand, Cranford[3] found that CAI in mathematics at the fifth grade and sixth grade levels had little effect on the students' understanding of basic mathematics concepts; however, both boys and girls achieved at a faster rate in mathematics computation and applications in the CAI program than in the traditional mathematics program. Barnes[4] studied the role of learner-controlled instruction in CAI by using six randomly assigned CAI drill-and-practice multiplication programs. The results indicated there were no significant differences in the results. Wilson and Fitzgibbon[5] reported significantly higher scores in English grammar, mechanics, and usage by the CAI group in a study that involved an elementary English drill-and-practice program. Fletcher and Atkinson[6] studied CAI use in reading at kindergarten through third grade levels. They found that both

Elementary school CAI gets their attention.

boys and girls benefitted from the CAI instruction in reading, though there was relatively more gain for boys than for girls from CAI experience. Atkinson[7] later reported on CAI efforts in teaching children to read in first grade, second grade, and third grade. As was found in the earlier Fletcher and Atkinson research, the CAI group did significantly better than the control group of students. Litman's[8] study of CAI reading drill and practice at fourth grade and fifth grade levels in selected Chicago schools showed that the CAI students scored significantly higher than the control group.

JUNIOR HIGH SCHOOL STUDIES

Hatfield[9] studied seventh grade mathematics course results and came to conflicting conclusions about the effect of CAI. The control group did better in the first year of the study, although the CAI group excelled in the second year of the study. A study by Crawford[10] researched CAI drill and practice with seventh grade remedial mathematics students. The CAI groups showed significant gains on the post-test scores after eight weeks of drill-and-practice work with the computer. The Wilkinson study[11] used an individualized CAI program with 195 black and Hispanic students in New York City. The Science Research Associates Achievement Series test used in the Wilkinson study yielded higher scores for CAI students in the mathematics, reading, and social studies subtests than for nonCAI students.

HIGH SCHOOL STUDIES

A study concerned with CAI tutorial instruction for high school chemistry was made by Summerlin.[12] Students in the control group scored better on the post-test than the CAI students. Sixty days later, the control group again scored better than the CAI group. Summerlin suggested shorter tutorial programs as a more effective and efficient use of CAI. Wolcott's study[13] of high school typewriting students found that the traditional method of instruction was as effective as the CAI method of instruction, except that students took longer to reach the same level of achievement using the traditional method. Pachter's research[14] was conducted with low-achieving ninth grade mathematics students using a CAI tutorial mode. The CAI group was more successful than the conventional group, possibly because learner interest was high and absenteeism was low.

SUMMARY COMMENT

These highlights on CAI research represent research conducted mainly with drill-and-practice and tutorial computer programs. More research needs to be conducted using some of the other computer instructional applications, such as simulation and problem-solving programs. However, from the findings of the research available, the assumption can be made that the microcomputer can be used effectively and efficiently at all grade levels, by all students, and in all disciplines.

WHAT BENEFITS FOR THE TEACHER?

CAI can be defined as use of the computer or microcomputer as a medium of instruction that is interactive and frequently individualized. CAI is often first used by teachers to assist in the task of giving information and in routine drill-and-practice lessons. This frees the teacher to provide more interpersonal socialization opportunities in the classroom and more small-group work with students. Use of CAI in the drill-and-practice mode gives a helping hand to many elementary teachers who conscientiously feel torn between the needs of some students for reinforcing practice and drill, and the needs of all the students for group experiences and the development of values and understanding.

Before considering the variety of possible benefits that CAI provides a teacher, it may be useful to set forth some definitions of what is involved in CAI and a microcomputer. CAI can be classified in terms of:

1. *Drill and practice* assumes that the subject matter of the lesson has been introduced and provides a repetitive question-and-answer format. Drill may involve rapid student response, such as in the use of flash cards. Questions and answers tend to be brief, in contrast to

What Benefits for the Teacher? 97

Accepting information

Storing information

Processing information

Distributing information

Many routine teacher functions can be performed by the microcomputer.

      practice formats, in which answers are of a more complex nature. The completion of multiple steps in the solution of a practice problem may be required.
2. *Tutor* involves the introduction of material to be learned, but often includes drill and practice. It is usually composed of text material with questions under the control of a branching set of rules that are responsive to the answers that are given.
3. *Simulation* attempts to simulate real life situations. The random events generated by the microcomputer are intro-

duced to depict the impact of alternative events on a social or scientific system. It is usually a very accurate replication of an event.
4. *Problem solving* with the computer is used as a tool for exploration, investigation, and clarification of problems. The user may write his or her own program as a solution is sought.
5. *CMI* is used to support teachers in the instructional process through the generation of tests, scoring, student record keeping, reports, and so forth. CMI is an instructional application that uses a computer system to store objectives, instructional materials inventory, evaluation criteria, and records of student achievement.

Imagine yourself as a second grade teacher or a fifth grade teacher. The typical teaching schedule that governs the Monday-through-Friday school experiences of teachers and students are displayed in the boxed sections that follow. Note that there is no time to spare. Where can the teacher benefit most from using a microcomputer? Where can microcomputer CAI lessons be of most value to students?

MICROCOMPUTER USE IN SECOND GRADE

Science and social studies each have only thirty minutes, every day of the week, in the second grade schedule. This does not leave time for individual time on a microcomputer, but does leave time for a class demonstration of a science or social studies simulation using a large video screen with the microcomputer. A similar demonstration, but with art or music software might be effectively used in the 30 minutes available on any of the four days that art and music are scheduled. The large-group computer approach can represent an enrichment of the teaching and learning experience in a second grade classroom.

In second grade, both reading and arithmetic have high priority in the time allotted. Reading is scheduled for 100 minutes (not counting the 60 minutes scheduled for the English, spelling, and handwriting periods). Arithmetic is scheduled for 55 minutes. If the second grade class of 29 pupils is divided into the five or six reading groups that might be expected, this means that each group has five or six pupils, and the class has a total of 600 minutes per week for reading activity. Suppose each group has six students; if you assign a pair of students to one of the three microcomputers with 20 minutes of microcomputer use for each pair of students or 10 minutes for each student, all five of the groups can have some microcomputer experience on any single class day. Experience has shown that 10 minutes of work on the microcomputer is an effective period of time, even at the second grade level. Ten minutes of activity tends to leave the student still wanting more time. The microcomputers are assumed to be available to any one class only on one day a week, thus three microcomputers can serve five classes per week with this kind of intensive experience.

A diagram of the microcomputer use pattern described above looks like this:

Micro #1   Micro #2   Micro #3
(S#1   S#2)   (S#3   S#4)   (S#5   S#6)
100 minutes/20 minutes (6 students) = 30 students

Although five second grades in a school might be rare in 1984, higher enrollment is expected after 1985. In some states, there are as few as 175 days of school per year or 35 weeks within which these second grade students might have a single day each week of microcomputer experience in reading reinforcement. Those 35 periods of ten minutes of per pupil microcomputer experience in a second grade reading class can make a significant difference. Practice and drill on reading skills with the microcomputer keeps the student on the task and working toward mastery of skills. Because 55 minutes for arithmetic is substantially less time than the 100 minutes for reading, less microcomputer work can be scheduled for your class of 29 students. On the basis of having three microcomputers for a single period per week, the opportunities for drill or problem solving will be half those in reading; thus each student can have ten minutes every two weeks instead of ten minutes each week.

SECOND GRADE DAILY SCHEDULE

> 8:30 Reading
> 10:10 Physical Education
> 10:35 Arithmetic—Learning Center (one day)
> 11:30 Lunch
> 12:30 Language Arts (English)
> 1:00 Art or Music (four days) Health (one day)
> 1:30 Spelling (three days) Handwriting (two days)
> 2:00 Social Studies
> 2:30 Science
> 3:00 End of day

MICROCOMPUTER USE IN FIFTH GRADE

The schedule given for the fifth grade reflects the partial departmentalization of subjects at that level in a suburban school. Of the four fifth grade teachers, one provides all the English instruction, a second provides all the science instruction, a third provides all the social studies instruction, while the fourth provides the creative writing, handwriting, and spelling aspects of composition. Each of the four teaches reading and mathematics. You will find the schedule set forth in the boxed exhibit that follows.

In these fifth grade classes, the division of the school day is as follows:

- English—40 minutes
- Science—40 minutes
- Social studies—40 minutes
- Composition—40 minutes
- Reading—50 minutes
- Mathematics—50 minutes
- Physical education—25 minutes
- Music and art—25 minutes
- Independent study period—20 minutes

What the time dimensions given above mean in terms of microcomputer use by students can be seen in comparing the fifth grade time portions to the second grade time plan already described. Both reading and mathematics now have the same time situation that mathematics had in the second grade schedule. English, science, social studies, and composition now have 40 percent of the amount of time that reading had in the second grade pattern. Thus, the total feasible microcomputer time for a fifth grade student in any of these subjects is 14 ten-minute periods during the 35 weeks of the school year. In a school where the teachers and the administration care about providing microcomputer learning experiences for students, having a total of 50 ten-minute periods in a year for each fifth grade student is an impressive total.

These 500 minutes per student are the result of allocating equipment as follows:

- 3 microcomputers for use in a class of thirty
- Reading use per student can equal 18 weeks of ten minutes each
- Mathematics use per student can equal 18 weeks of 10 minutes each
- English, science, social studies, and composition use per student can equal 14 weeks of ten minutes each

The 500 minutes of fifth grade student exposure to a microcomputer in a school year compares with the 530 minutes possible in the second grade school year. The benefit to any fifth grade teacher can be measured not only in terms of the student enrichment this makes possible, but also in terms of the lesson makeup and lesson reinforcement that can now be delegated to the CMI capabilities of a microcomputer. Each school will have to come to terms with its own instructional priorities, its space limitations, and the degree of scheduling cooperation possible between teachers of different grades and subject matter. The potential for providing a new and exciting experience in learning for the fifth grade teacher can be very real.

Teachers in a more departmentalized setting will probably realize that much of what applies in a situation like the fifth grade schedule given above will apply in a departmentalized schedule. Some teachers will agree that CAI integrates readily into the teaching and learning schedule, yet want to incorporate some programming experiences into their students' classroom experiences. Without question, adding a new subject to the curriculum, like programming in LOGO, in PILOT, or in BASIC, will require classroom time that has been allocated to some other subject in the daily schedule. Such a problem is not new in education and the answer will be found in the same way that new subject matter was added to the curriculum in years past.

FIFTH GRADE DAILY SCHEDULE

8:30 Physical Education
8:55 Music or Art
9:20 Mathematics
10:10 Social Studies
10:50 Science
11:30 Lunch Period
12:30 Reading
1:20 Language Arts (English)
2:00 Composition (spelling, handwriting, writing)
2:40 Independent Study Period
3:00 End of day

The case for CAI and the benefits it provides teachers and students are reported in the teacher experiences in the following paragraphs. The most praised aspect of CAI and the use of a microcomputer in teaching is the individualization that teachers report using. Conscientious teachers have been frustrated by the difficulty of individualizing materials and learning for their students. Just remembering where to find the material the teacher earlier identified as likely to be beneficial for an individual student is a challenge. Instruction with branching capabilities to review lessons when needed or to move a student ahead when ready can be delivered by the microcomputer more easily, and with much less fatigue, than by any teacher; this in itself is a strong recommendation for use of the CAI microcomputer as a classroom tool.

Teachers report weak students making more progress and average students surprising themselves with good results through CAI lessons. One teacher remarked that it was enough to give him an inferiority complex, that after months of trying to reach a student of very limited ability, the microcomputer seemed to unlock the learning capacity like magic. Another teacher credited the high motivation students experience as the secret ingredient to microcomputer CAI use. After all, she reasons, the microcomputer is part of the student's era, it has some of the same mystique video games have. Whatever the reasons, teachers are nearly unanimous in reporting sharply upgraded student performance and high motivation.

Although teachers are pleased with any help they can get in improving student learning performance, the most often cited benefit of a microcomputer from the teacher's standpoint is the evaluation of student's strengths and weaknesses. Such diagnosis is not limited to subjects like mathematics, but includes a wide range of diagnostics in English composition and reading. The privacy and speed with which the microcomputer with an appropriate software program can involve a student in completing the diagnostic routine is especially valued by teachers in their reports. The microcomputer's ability to provide immediate feedback, not just in a diagnostic mode, but in all of its uses, is one of the most appreciated benefits according to teachers from coast to coast.

The microcomputer can help a teacher work with the special education staff in developing the individualized education plans (IEPs) needed and required for such students. The word-processing power as well as the CAI capabilities of a microcomputer can be of significant assistance in the development of special education programs.

The single, most important benefit is expressed in this way by a veteran with 20 years of experience in elementary teaching:

> I can now be the student's friend. I can coach my students and not be just a judge and jury! The microcomputer gives me the chance to encourage students, to provide suggestions, rather than constantly correct them. The microcomputer does the correcting and the students don't seem to

mind. When I do the correcting, there seems to be a constant battle.

These are important results in effective performance of the teaching and learning task faced by teachers in the classroom. When teachers see the benefits of using microcomputers in their classroom teaching, the introduction of microcomputers into the school will be viewed as an aid and not an intrusion of just one more thing to fit into an already crowded day. The challenge of the microcomputer age is that teachers and administrators find the ways to use these new tools effectively.

WHAT BENEFITS FOR THE STUDENT?

The availability of microcomputer CAI for a student means he or she can experience some unique benefits as part of the school day. The first benefit of direct importance to the student is the opportunity CAI provides for reinforcement of lessons not mastered when they were first presented. Teachers often realize that some students have not mastered the material presented, but it is too much to expect that students will diagnose their own needs. The records of the teacher should provide this insight, but too often those records omit details of learning components and record only the overall performance. The special advantage of CAI and CMI in a microcomputer teaching and learning situation is that each objective can be tested and the outcome can be recorded. Although some students may not consider the extent of information available about their performance as representing a benefit to them, the fact is that mastery of each learning objective is important to their personal growth.

If the microcomputer and CAI can play an important role in student learning reinforcement, it has an even more beneficial role to play in serving the absentee student. Far too often, absentees are made to feel that they are imposing on the time and good nature of the teacher when asking for help on the material presented during their absence. Absentees frequently do impose a hardship on the teacher, as well as on themselves. The microcomputer and a CAI lesson that parallels the content of the text can present the instruction missed, test mastery of the material, and record readiness to proceed with classroom materials. In one school, this process is carried on in a learning-center situation where the classroom teacher sends the student upon their return from absence with a note on what lesson material was missed. The learning-center aide inserts the appropriate disk in the microcomputer disk drive and the absentee can then proceed to learn the material and respond at his or her own pace.

For many students, the most exciting and rewarding part of access to CAI programs is the opportunity to pursue special concepts in a given subject matter to a much greater extent than a classroom learning situation makes possible. The provision by many schools for learning by their gifted students has been exemplary. Now such enriched learning opportunities can be made readily available, with students setting the pace for themselves as to how far they pursue the learning opportunity presented. Although some students may have interests that go beyond the limits of program material available for their use in a given school, the ever increasing quantity of high quality courseware suggests that there need not be a limit on student learning of advanced concepts for long.

Finally, as students move through the school system and as they turn their attention to career opportunities and to college study possibilities, the microcomputer can be of special benefit. A number of the major career selection programs, which were once available only on a time-sharing mainframe computer network, are now available in microcomputer format. Where a particular time-sharing career guidance program is not yet available in microcomputer format, the microcomputer can be used in place of the terminal to access regional and national career and college databases. In addition, the role of the microcomputer in providing for significant tutorial help and drill and practice assistance on the Scholastic Aptitude Test (S.A.T.) and advanced placement tests is just beginning to be realized. The high school student will come to regard the microcomputer as a very useful tool in making career choices, and in specific preparation for college entrance tests.

WHAT BENEFIT FOR THE ADMINISTRATOR?

The special benefits of CAI and microcomputers for administrators is found in their response capabilities to some of the thorny issues that confront the school principal, the curriculum coordinator, and the superintendent's office. These are the issues of mandated programs, programs for the gifted, bilingual programs, and programs for the handicapped.

A mandate might concern providing career education for all students or only some students. One of the constant problems of the administrator is how and where to find materials about the world of work that are more useful to students than the limited insight provided by teachers who have never held any other job. The problem with textbook material and study materials is that they are often out of date and lack impact on the student reader. The experience of MECC in providing "Selling Lemonade" is revealing. It is so popular and so adaptable to the varying ages of students that the Apple Computer Company adopted this program as one of the sample programs they provide on their master system disk. "Lemonade Stand" represents a serious look at how the world of business exists. Yet students from first grade on through high school find it a fascinating challenge. These students have no idea how sound a foundation in marketing, production, and finance they are being exposed to. You can discover a wide variety of microcomputer programs aimed at other mandated elements of the teaching and learning program of your school by searching out the courseware catalogs listing available programs for your brand of microcomputer.

The usefulness of the microcomputer in providing enriched study materials for gifted students should require little comment in light of the previous discussion of the benefit to students these microcomputer programs represent. Every administrator has to be concerned with the cost effectiveness of each component in the district's education program. There do not seem to be any studies yet on the cost effectiveness of microcomputer responses to the needs of gifted students, but

CAI works with all ages.

the experience of teachers and administrators who have used microcomputers in this way suggests that the costs, when compared with the learning results, are far from prohibitive.

There are a growing number of microcomputer programs that respond to the needs of the bilingual student and to the needs of the handicapped student. The Material Resource list in the Appendix gives a number of these special resources. One teacher of non-English-speaking students reported high success in giving students a simple word-processing program and requiring them to write English sentences using the microcomputer keyboard, then printing their work on a printer so that the students could have a printed copy of what they had created. Their pride in the English sentences they had typed into the microcomputer keyboard was something to see. Teachers who have worked with a variety of handicapped students report a similar pride in their achievements using a microcomputer. The microcomputer's capacity to recognize speech, to speak words and sentences, and to accept light pen and other screen-touching inputs makes it a very productive learning tool for handicapped students. Where patience is so important an ingredient in teaching and learning, the microcomputer excels.

In addition to the special instructional concerns of the administrator, the microcomputer is especially valuable in helping with record keeping and planning. The microcomputer can provide almost every record-keeping function for small- and middle-size school districts that large school districts have previously accomplished on mainframe computers. Some of the educational administration applications already available for one brand of microcomputer or another are listed below:

- Athletics
- Attendance records
- Budgeting, accounting, and other business management software—district and building levels
- Grade analysis and reporting
- Guidance
- Instructional management
- Inventory and property records
- Media center records
- Planning and scheduling
- Staff personnel records
- Student records

These 11 kinds of administrative records are already being kept on microcomputers in some districts through the use of software created especially for educational administrative use.

The latest developments in microcomputer use for educational administrators are represented by the Apple "LISA" and the integrated software for the IBM-PC and other brands of microcomputers. These programs provide easy access to and transfer of data from a database program to an electronic spreadsheet to a graph-creating program, and even on to a word-processing program without the necessity of re-entering any data. The ability to enter data just once, and then be able to use that data in a variety of ways, is a major aid in the conduct of educational administration.

SUMMARY

Research done on mainframe-computer use of CAI suggests that there is a measurable benefit to be gained from using CAI in a wide range of grade levels, in many subjects, and in many parts of the country. More research is presently underway on microcomputer use of CAI and the consequences for learning that can be expected.

Teachers directly benefit from microcomputer CAI use in the school through the individualization and immediate feedback made possible and from the upgrading of student performance reported that accompanies microcomputer use. Both the motivational aspects and diagnostic capabilities of microcomputer use are praised by teachers. Perhaps the greatest benefit to teachers is the teacher's role change that the use of CAI makes possible. The change from the role of critic and judge to that of ally and partner in learning is welcomed by teachers.

Students seem to be enthusiastic about the ability of a microcomputer to let them go beyond the limits of the classroom instruction to investigate concepts and subject matter of special interest. There is also enthusiasm about the CAI capability of providing learning reinforcement for the student who does not master the material when it is first presented, as well as about CAI's ability to provide instructional assistance to the returning absentee.

Administrators are finding the microcomputer and CAI useful in serving some of the state-mandated programs and especially in providing enriched learning materials for gifted students. The potential of CAI for bilingual and handicapped education has only begun to be appreciated. Administrators are finding the microcomputer a helpful adjunct in their administration of a school district. The record-keeping abilities of the microcomputer are sufficient for many small- and medium-size districts. School superintendents report that

the breadth of specialized programs already available provides most of the administrative answers needed.
NOTE TO THE TEACHER: Although the Activities provided at the end of Chapter four are primarily for your use, the first two Activities given below have been used successfully with some students.

ACTIVITY ONE

MODIFYING A CAI PROGRAM

1. OBJECTIVE:
The teacher will be able to modify a program by changing the DATA lines.

2. TEACHER PREPARATION:
The "Spell-N-Time" program of the School Courseware Journal is widely available (see Activity Five in Chapter two). You may find that your school already has a copy. The program has been translated so that it will run on every major brand of microcomputer. The spelling list may be changed daily, weekly, or whenever new spelling words need to be added or whenever the words mastered by students deleted. Also, the teacher controls the number of words to be presented during each "game." To make those changes follow the directions on pages 3 through 5 of the *Spell-N-Time* documentation for your brand of microcomputer.

3. TEACHER INSTRUCTIONS:
Follow the directions for your brand of microcomputer in loading the program and interrupting the running of the program so that you can LIST the line numbers as indicated on pages 4 and 5. First delete the DATA statements. Type in the line numbers for the lines on which you want to make a change, the word DATA, and then type in the new spelling word with hyphens as shown in the example found in the middle of page 5. When you have completed the retyping of any line, press the ENTER or RETURN key. You are then ready to type in the next

> line number, the word DATA, and the new hyphenated words for that line. When you have made all the changes in words you desire, be sure to save the program under a new name.

ACTIVITY TWO

CONVERTING A STORYBOARD TO A PROGRAM

1. OBJECTIVE:
The teacher will be able to convert a storyboard into a program using an authoring system or the PILOT language.

2. TEACHER PREPARATION:
You will need to prepare a storyboard series of twenty to thirty individual 3 × 5 cards (referred to as a "frame") that depict a short tutorial lesson on a subject relevant to your students (see the storyboard illustration in Chapter three as well as the text that begins with the AUTHORING SYSTEMS FOR CAI PROGRAMS section). Your choice of how your storyboard program is to be written for your microcomputer will be governed by whether you have available on authoring system or the PILOT language. You may wonder why you don't use BASIC. BASIC will require as much as ten times more "total developmental time" than will the use of an authoring system or PILOT as the programming approach. If you must use BASIC, cut the storyboard to not more than 20 individual 3 × 5 cards.

3. TEACHER INSTRUCTIONS:
Convert the storyboard into a microcomputer program, one frame at a time. Because authoring systems provide more extensive record-keeping capabilities than are usually programmable in PILOT, it will be desirable to keep any record-keeping to a minimum when using the PILOT language. You will want a record of the student name, the

problem attempted, and the number of attempts made before the student gives the correct answer.

The note at the beginning of the Activities for this chapter suggests that each of the first two activities can be used with students. If you have doubts about having students engage in these activities consider these factors:

1. Teachers report it works well
2. Students respond enthusiastically as this gives them a chance to show off their skills without detracting from your role as the teacher
3. Students who engage in translating a storyboard to program format will learn the material more thoroughly than in any other way

ACTIVITY THREE

EVALUATING SOFTWARE PROGRAMS

1. OBJECTIVE:
The teacher will be able to use an evaluation process to review and evaluate the usefulness of a microcomputer program for classroom use.

2. TEACHER PREPARATION:
You will need to obtain an evaluation form from one of the sources given and apply the criteria listed to the program you select to evaluate. You will discover that a thorough evaluation of most programs requires running the program more than once.

3. TEACHER INSTRUCTIONS:
Fill in all the sections of the evaluation form that you have selected for use. When you complete the form, decide whether you want to use the program in your class. It may help you if you assign yourself the writing of a report to your principal on why you will or will not be using the program you have evaluated. Completed evaluation forms

will also be useful to other teachers if they are kept in a central place for reference.

ACTIVITY FOUR

CREATING A WORKSHEET OR QUIZ

1. OBJECTIVE:
The teacher will be able to create a worksheet or quiz with a word-processing program and use a printer for printed copies of the worksheet or quiz.

2. TEACHER INSTRUCTIONS:
Use a word-processing program to create the worksheet or quiz by typing the quiz or worksheet on the microcomputer keyboard. When you have composed the material you want to print, first SAVE the word-processing file with a name that you will remember on a utility disk, and then print the worksheet or quiz. You may find that once you see it in print there are changes you want to make. These editing changes, such as moving, inserting, and deleting, can be made easily without retyping pages of material. After making the changes, SAVE the word processing file again, using the same name unless you have some reason to save both versions. Then print the revised version.

ACTIVITY FIVE

USING "QUIZSTAT"

1. OBJECTIVE:
The teacher will be able to use the "Quizstat" program to analyze the differences in students' responses in a quiz or test.

2. TEACHER PREPARATION:

You will need to obtain a copy of the "Quizstat" program. Because this program is included with the "Spell-N-Time" program used in Activity Five in Chapter two, it is probably already available in your school. After you have given a quiz to a class, follow the directions in the documentation for the "Quizstat" program.

3. TEACHER INSTRUCTIONS:

With the "Quizstat" program in the disk drive, type RUN QUIZSTAT and press RETURN or ENTER. Answer the questions that appear on the screen. Scan each student paper and type the quiz question number that was missed on each student's paper. Press the RETURN or ENTER key after each number typed. When you have finished typing the last quiz question number of the last student's paper in the group, type DONE and press RETURN or ENTER. The microcomputer will provide you with a printed or screen analysis of the number and percentage of students missing each question, the class average overall, and a grade percent scale.

NOTES

1. Suppes P, Morningstar M. Computer-Assisted Instruction. *Science.* October 17, 1969, pp. 343–350.
2. Harris R T. An evaluation of computer assisted instruction in mathematics using test-and-practice method for third and sixth grade students (PhD dissertation, United States International University, 1976). Abstracted in: *Dissertation Abstracts International,* 38 (Ann Arbor: University Microfilms International, 1977), 1245A.
3. Cranford H R. A study of the effects of computer-assisted instruction in mathematics on the achievement and attitude of pupils in grades five and six in a rural setting" (EdD dissertation, University of Southern Mississippi, 1976). Abstracted in: *Dissertation Abstracts International,* 37 (Ann Arbor: University Microfilms International, 1977), 5660A.
4. Barnes O D. The effect of learner controlled computer-assisted

instruction on performance in multiplication skills (PhD dissertation, University of Southern California, 1970). Abstracted in: *Dissertation Abstracts International*, 31 (Ann Arbor: University Microfilms International, 1971), 4538A.
5. Wilson H A, Fitzgibbon N H. Practice and perfection: A preliminary analysis of achievement data from the CAI elementary English program. *Elementary English*. April, 1970, pp. 576-579.
6. Fletcher J D, Atkinson R C. Evaluation of the Stanford CAI program in initial reading. *Journal of Educational Psychology*. December, 1972, pp. 597-602.
7. Atkinson R C. Teaching children to read using a computer. *American Psychologist*. March, 1974, pp. 169-178.
8. Litman G H. Relation between computer-assisted instruction and reading achievement among fourth, fifth, and sixth grade students (EdD dissertation, Northern Illinois University, 1977).
9. Hatfield L L. Computer-assisted mathematics: An investigation of the effectiveness of the computer used as a tool to learn mathematics (PhD dissertation, University of Minnesota, 1969). Abstracted in: *Dissertation Abstracts International*, 30 (Ann Arbor: University Microfilms International, 1970), 4329-4330A.
10. Crawford A N. A pilot study of computer-assisted drill and practice in seventh grade remedial mathematics. *California Journal of Educational Research*. September, 1970, pp. 170-181.
11. Wilkinson J H. The effectiveness of an individualized, computer-assisted instructional program (PLAN) with students from a low socio-economic community (PhD dissertation, St. John's University, 1979). Abstracted in: *Dissertation Abstracts International*, 40 (Ann Arbor: University Microfilms International, 1979), 1889A.
12. Summerlin L R. A feasibility study of tutorial type computer assisted instruction in selected topics in high school chemistry (PhD dissertation, University of Maryland, 1971). Abstracted in: *Dissertation Abstracts International*, 32 (Ann Arbor: University Microfilms International, 1972), 5636A.
13. Wolcott J M. The effect of computer-assisted instruction, traditional instruction and locus of control on achievement of beginning typewriting students (EdD dissertation, Temple University, 1976). Abstracted in: *Dissertation Abstracts International*, 37 (Ann Arbor: University Microfilms International, 1976), 1942A.

14. Pachter S N. A computer assisted tutorial module for teaching the factoring of second degree polynomials to regents level ninth year mathematics students (EdD dissertation, Columbia University Teachers College, 1979). Abstracted in: *Dissertation Abstracts International*, 40 (Ann Arbor, University Microfilms International, 1979), 1843A.

5

WHAT ELSE CAN A MICROCOMPUTER DO FOR INSTRUCTION?

If you have concluded that microcomputers may be fine for instruction, possibly even a real help to the conscientious teacher, you may still be thinking, "What can the microcomputer do for me?" And so, last but not least, you can read about the possibilities microcomputers have for your record-keeping and other nonteaching duties. There are some programs that make classroom record keeping almost pleasant. These programs are generally database programs that can readily be structured for almost any form of record keeping. There are also some specialized programs with names like "Gradebook" and "Teacher's Aid" that are simply very small, specialized database programs.

Because the word "database" has been used twice in the previous paragraph, perhaps it is time to define the term. "Database" is the computer term for a series of records. You can think of it as a large four-drawer file cabinet, with 50 file folders in each drawer, and perhaps as many as ten individual letters or documents in each file folder. These numbers are arbitrary. The number of file drawers, file folders, and letters could be larger or smaller. What is important to understand about a database is that it is no more mysterious than your memo book and the information you have recorded in it.

Most teachers begin with an inexpensive, specialized "Gradebook" type of program that will run in the brand of microcomputer at school. You can obtain the essence of what such a program will accomplish, as a substitute for the typical gradebook, in the paragraphs that follow. No doubt you will find there are some records you will want to keep that do not fit in the microcomputer record-keeping program you purchased. Yes, you will probably buy that first recordkeeping program with your own money! Perhaps you will be advised that the school has bought or will buy a database program, but at the beginning, the task of entrusting your gradebook records to the "big" program will be more than you are willing to undertake. Furthermore, you will probably use both your regular gradebook and the microcomputer gradebook program, side-by-side, for the first semester, or even a year. When you finally switch over to the fancier database program, for a while you will keep records in both your regular gradebook and on the database you created.

Why would you bother to use the microcomputer with a gradebook program and still keep your grade records in the regular gradebook? The duplication in time and effort is the price you pay for not being sure of the microcomputer and your use of it. As a matter of fact, even the manufacturers of the fancy large computers routinely urge accounting departments to keep their accounting records in the usual way when they first adopt and are getting used to a new, larger computer. Once you have become accustomed to using a microcomputer for your classroom record keeping, you will wonder why you didn't discover this easier way to more complete and useful records earlier.

HOW CAN A GRADEBOOK PROGRAM HELP?

The typical gradebook program will cost as little as $20 or as much as $100. In contrast, database programs can cost as much as $700. Some specialized school recordkeeping programs will run to as much as $5,000. Consider the following report provided by teachers who have used a grade recordkeeping program. The program is capable of providing a student directory, processing grades, and providing a seating assignment listing. There is a provision in the student directory for entering the student's name, parent's name, home phone number, the student's homeroom teacher's name, the student's birthday, the student's seat number, a record of absences and tardinesses, a record of any loan of school materials to the student, and a record of the student return of the report card. Additional student directory categories can be determined by the individual teacher and used as needed.

Once the complete student directory is prepared, the program provides for three "seat assignment" functions. First, you can discover the seat assignment you made when you created the student directory. But, if a seat assignment was not given to each student at the time the student directory was created, now you can do so in either of two ways. You may simply assign students to seat numbers of your choice or instruct the microcomputer to make a random assignment of students to the seats in the classroom. Microcomputer random assignment is a popular choice because it frees the teacher of any feeling of bias in the seat assignment process. Also, the gradebook program makes possible changes in seating from the random seat assignments if the teacher needs to over-ride the microcomputer assignment because of potential discipline or learning difficulties such as hearing deficiencies or eyesight problems.

The most useful aspect of the gradebook program is in the recording of grades. The grade-recording section provides for five separate grade-recording files, such as Language Arts, Arithmetic, Science, Social Studies, and Art or Music. The choice of subject is recorded in each of the five categories created by the teacher. Within a given subject field, the teacher can use the program segment called "entering student scores" and the microcomputer screen displays the names of the students previously listed in the student directory section of the program, in alphabetic order. The raw score for the student's work is then typed and entered. The next name is then displayed and the teacher enters the raw score and presses ENTER again. If a student has missed the assignment or test due to an absence, the teacher records the lack of a grade by pressing ENTER. By entering a zero and then pressing ENTER, the teacher may penalize the student because of an unexcused absence. When the last student's raw score has been typed in, followed by ENTER, the microcomputer displays the grades, rearranged from highest to lowest. The teacher can make notes on the lowest A, lowest B, etcetera, and then press ENTER to see a display of an automatically calculated percentile grade displayed along with the arithmetic mean of the raw scores. If the teacher follows this by calling for the part of the program that permits assigning letter grades, the microcomputer screen will display a bar chart of the grade distribution. Pressing ENTER brings to the screen a listing of each student, the letter grade earned, the raw score, and the grade points (on a 4.0 scale). Finally, the records created are then filed by the microcomputer. An especially useful feature of the program is the ability to retrieve a single student's grade record. This capability means that the teacher no longer has to be concerned about an individual student inquiring about a grade and inadvertently seeing the grades of other students. Another helpful feature of the program, as reported by two junior high school teachers, is the ability to weight the various grade categories, so that in Language Arts, for example, records can be set up for grammar, composition, spelling, reading, and literature. One teacher gave a weight of two each to composition, reading, and grammar, with a weight of one each for spelling and literature. This resulted not only in calculations for each individual component subject, but a weighted grade for the Language Arts performance of each student. This was particularly helpful when report cards were prepared.

READABILITY EVALUATIONS AND OTHER ANALYTIC USES

Most teachers have observed the frustration exhibited by some students when reading the assigned textbook or other print materials. This frustration often suggests that the reading level of the text does not match the reading ability of the student. Conscientious teachers who are concerned about students' success in reading will find themselves involved in the time-consuming task of counting syllables, words, sentences, and unfamiliar words so that a readability formula may be used. This is a lot of work, as any teacher who has tried it knows. The possibility of missing a word in the word

Readability Evaluations and Other Analytic Uses 121

There are computer programs to evaluate the reading level of texts to see if it matches the ability of students.

count, or a syllable in those formulas that call for syllable counts, is very high. Any interruption can require starting the count all over again. One of the special advantages of microcomputer programs is that there are programs that can perform tasks better than any human. An example of this capability is represented by the microcomputer programs that provide readability analysis. Although such programs vary in the formula approach they use, they are alike in the simplicity of typing text of a selected 100-word passage on the keyboard of the microcomputer. Any interruption of the task does not mean starting over, it just means continuing to type words from the text into the microcomputer. When the text input has been completed, the readability analysis program takes over. A readability program that is the result of work by Dr. Max Jerman is available for various brands of microcomputers. It is sold by several publishers who serve as distributors for this readability analysis, as well as by Dr. Jerman's own firm.[1] The Jerman readability analysis program offers grade-level estimates of the typed text passage in terms of the following:

1. Flesch readability formula
2. Fog index
3. Dale-Chall readability formula
4. SMOG grade
5. Wheeler-Smith readability formula
6. Spache readability formula

Two levels of analysis may be requested when using the Jerman program. The first analysis segment is for the primary level. This analysis, which appears on the screen, provides (1) a listing and a count of all the words in the text sample that are not found on the Dale-Chall "easy word list," (2) an application of the Wheeler-Smith formula, and (3) an application of the Spache formula when the nature of the text permits its use.

The second analysis segment is appropriate for reading levels of grade four through adult. This analysis gives results for the Dale-Chall readability formula, the Fog index, the Flesch readability formula, the SMOG Grade, and an average of the Dale-Chall, Fog, and Flesch indices. A typical screen display might look like the illustration below:

REGULAR ANALYSIS (GR 4—ADULT)
1. DALE-CHALL   8.2
2. FOG INDEX   12.8
3. FLESCH GRADE LEVEL   9.5
4. SMOG INDEX   9.3
PRESS RETURN TO CONTINUE

One of the special features of the Jerman program is that, in addition to the primary grade analysis and the analysis for grades four through adult, the teacher can ask for "complete statistics," which yields a screen full of information. The number of sentences in the text sample, the number of letters typed in the text sample, the average number of letters per word, and the number of words having more than two syllables are set forth on the screen with the formula results revealed by the analysis.

An interesting capability of the Jerman program is shown in the "display of words of more than two syllables." Because the English language has some words that do not follow standard syllabication rules, the Jerman readability analysis program will show words in the listing of "more than two syllables" that do not belong in that category. The Jerman program adapts to this situation by adjusting the formulas that use a syllable count accordingly. In addition to a screen listing of words of more than two syllables, the teacher can call for a listing of words that do not appear on the Dale list of 3,000 commonly used words. This is a slow process because each word in the text sample must be compared with the 3,000-word memory file. One of the most time-consuming steps involves providing a list of all the words of the text sample, listed in alphabetic order.

Three special commands in the Jerman readability analysis program may be of interest to classroom teachers. These are the commands that permit "changing a stat," "changing a word," and "adding a word." The effect of each of these commands is that the teacher can see what would happen if some change in the sample text were made. For example, in creating print material for a unit, the teacher might want to know what would change the text sample from the seventh grade readability level reported by the Jerman analysis, to the fifth grade level that is the target for which the unit is written. The program permits consideration of whether changing from longer to shorter sentences or changing from polysyllabic words to shorter words will be more useful in changing the readability level from seventh grade to fifth grade. Once the "change stat" evaluation has been made, the teacher writing a unit has the opportunity to actually "change words" or "add words" to the sample text earlier typed on the microcomputer keyboard. The use of these three special commands makes readjusting written material to a desired level a manageable task. Although, to our knowledge, the use of these three capabilities to assist students in improving their writing has not been explored, this would seem to be a promising technique for students who want to improve the level of their written compositions.

There are readability analysis programs available for a variety of microcomputers. One unique program exists that permits the use of a readability analysis linked to the composition of students using a word-processing program. This program makes it possible to create a theme or paragraph by students, then the analysis of the student's written work by a readability analysis program. The special value of the "word processing then readability approach" is that the word-processing program provides greater flexibility in composing the text and in changing any part of the text. Furthermore, the "word processing then readability approach" makes it possible to print the student composition on a microcomputer printer. The pride of student writers in their printed copy is something to behold. The high motivation for improvement in written composition created by the "word processing then readability analysis approach" suggests that the process merits further exploration.

Other analytical programs available for a variety of microcomputers are useful for teachers. For example, sometimes

Students enjoy seeing their own words "in print."

teachers want to do an analysis of questions missed on a student test. The frequency of incorrect answers to a given question can suggest the need for reinforcement of student understanding, or the need to rewrite the question, or both. However, unless the test results are analyzed, the need for change or reinforcement will not be realized. Analysis of questions missed on a test has frequently been viewed as a desirable thing to do, but something teachers can seldom fit into their busy schedules. In addition to providing specific item analysis of questions missed, this program provides the teacher with a count of students missing each question, the percentage of students missing each question, the class average overall, and a grade-percent scale. Furthermore, quizzes and examinations do not have to be multiple choice, true-false, or machine markable. To use the program, the teacher simply reviews each student paper, after it has been marked for errors, and types on the microcomputer keyboard each question number that the student answered incorrectly. When there are no more papers to enter, the teacher types DONE, presses the RETURN or ENTER key and the microcomputer does the rest. The program provides an option of viewing the results on the screen or in printed form. The output identifies the question number and the number of students who missed that question, the percentage of students who missed the question, and highlights those problems that fifty percent or more of the students answered incorrectly. Because grading tests of more than ten questions can be tedious with a class of thirty or more students, to expect a teacher to then analyze the questions that were particularly troubling to the students may be less than is realistic. This kind of analytic program can make the microcomputer a strong ally of good teaching.

 Another kind of microcomputer program that aids the teacher in the noninstructional aspects of classroom duties is found in the word-processing programs described in Chapter three. Microcomputer catalogs list a number of specialized programs that permit creating short notes to parents or students, and some of these programs may be very easy to use, but it seems more sensible for a teacher to use a word processing program than to invest even the $39.95 involved in buying the special, but limited, program. Teachers have found the "global search" capability of many word processing programs to be very helpful. For example, if a teaching objective or reference to a teaching resource has been listed on a disk using the word-processing program, the search command will find the specific words in the title, sentence, phrase, or other expression, saving the time and frustration of trying to hunt through files for the elusive reference or learning objective.

A variety of choices are available in microcomputer catalogs for "quiz writing" programs. These programs often make it possible to create text for a tutorial lesson, followed by a quiz over the material presented. The programs will do what they say, but the same effort spent learning how to use PILOT as an authoring language (discussed in Chapter three), or the same effort spent in learning how to use "BLOCKS," CAIware, or "Author I," may result in greater returns to a teacher. In general, more comprehensive programs will be worth the extra effort of learning how to use them because they will permit the creation of things that are important to effective classroom management.

CURRICULUM DESIGN AND DEVELOPMENT: CHALLENGE FOR TEACHERS

Microcomputers are effectively used in all subject areas with all types of students and at all grade levels. Thus the infusion of microcomputer use into the curriculum as a supplementary aid to instruction seems to be a realistic goal. Arthur Combs, writing in the *Phi Delta Kappan*, suggests that the educational community "must concentrate on growth and development of persons rather than on content and subject matter."[2] After citing the developments in this information age, Combs makes the point that the same curriculum cannot be required of everyone and that the curriculum must become increasingly individual in its impact and personal in its application. If microcomputers are to be used in the classroom as a tool for the personal application of curriculum for students, the classroom teacher must be involved in creating a learning climate where microcomputers are used to individualize learning for students. This is a new and awesome challenge.

When thinking about the microcomputer's role in instruction, it does not mean thinking about the microcomputer but thinking about instruction.[3] An issue that emerges is whether the role of microcomputer instruction should be one of infusion or of unit integration. Infusion can be defined as putting computer literacy objectives into all areas of the existing curriculum at the same time and using whatever materials and equipment are available.[4] On the other hand, unit integration involves introducing computer literacy into one area of the curriculum at a time.[5] The major advocate of the infusion approach is the Human Resources Research Organization (Hum/RRO). The HumRRO position is worthy of study by any teacher or administrator concerned with the role of the microcomputer in education. The infusion process may be more traumatic for elementary teachers because, unlike the unit integration approach, the infusion approach assumes that teachers can cope with microcomputer instructional use in every area of their teaching.

Your potential role in using a microcomputer as an aid to your students' learning process is likely to involve some blend of the unit integration approach with what your school district leadership may later mandate as an infusion process. What are the real requirements you may face? While the challenge will differ with the grade levels or the subject areas of your teaching expertise, there are some guidelines to consider that already exist. *Electronic Learning*[6] presented a series of scope and sequence models spanning the range of Kindergarten through grade 12. This series, authored by Dr. Gary Bitter of Arizona State University, should be required reading for every teacher concerned with the challenge of curriculum design in the context of including microcomputer literacy in the curriculum. Fundamental to any concern about microcomputer instructional use is a clear understanding of (1) the microcomputer as a tool to be used in the learning process, and of (2) the microcomputer as the object of a student's learning experience. The thrust of the Bitter series, cited above, is on understanding the microcomputer as an object of learning through computer awareness and programming.

A slightly different approach is provided by a revised K-8 computer literacy curriculum from the Cupertino Union School District.[7] Unlike Bitter's work, this curriculum is the outcome of a year of classroom experience and the revisions that appeared to be needed. The Cupertino curriculum lists a number of curriculum objectives to be introduced, expanded, or reinforced for grade levels Kindergarten through eight. Computer literacy in the Cupertino approach involves introducing, expanding, and reinforcing student understanding in computer awareness, computer-programming skills, social sciences, language arts, science, and mathematics. Many classroom teachers report that the microcomputer becomes part of a student's awareness through their use of this "teaching machine" in the pursuit of subject matter lessons. If this is true for your teaching situation, how will your curriculum be affected?

First, you can become familiar with the microcomputer teaching resources that your school has on hand for use, will buy from publishers, can borrow from other in-district schools, and can borrow from cooperative consortia. You may be amazed to discover the number of microcomputer instructional programs available if you begin asking your fellow teachers, your curriculum supervisor, and even the data

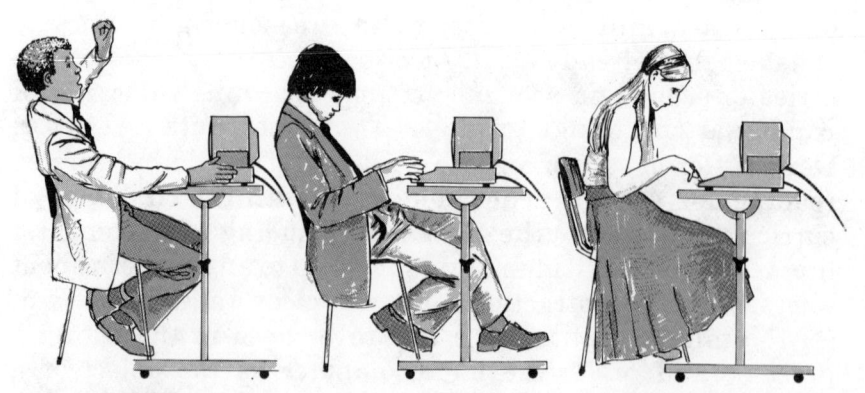

Increasing computer literacy through the use of microcomputers as teaching machines.

processing manager in the district office. Finding other sources for software will entail (1) writing to publishers, (2) looking for microcomputer exhibits at professional meetings, (3) talking with teachers in other schools about resources they have found, (4) carefully reading the professional magazines and the educational microcomputer magazines for articles, software reviews, and advertisements that can provide you with clues on microcomputer programs that will fit your teaching style and the kind of students you have in your classroom, (5) contacting the state office of education personnel for information, and (6) contacting teacher centers or other local cooperative educational organizations.

As you become familiar with the use of microcomputer programs available for instruction, you will also discover a significant issue that divides the publishing and educational community. This is the issue of what license the vendor of microcomputer courseware conveys to the buyer. Can your district buy a particular microcomputer program for use in your school, in your grade, and then loan it to another school, even another grade in your school? The attitude of some publishers has been expressed quite clearly in their edict that a diskette cannot be used except in the classroom for which it was bought. You may think this is ridiculous, yet that is the meaning of the fine print in the license agreement that accompanies many software programs. You are aware that the textbooks you are using in your classroom this year may be reissued to another school in the district next year. Nonetheless, you will find that some publishers are requiring special district-wide fees be paid if a microcomputer program is to be used in more than a single location. It seems only good sense to insist that what the school district buys for one school can be used in any school of the system, just as books have been treated for many years. Furthermore, if a cooperative consortium of school districts purchases instructional software, the same principle of sharing this resource between schools in the consortium should follow. Teachers have certainly borrowed films from regional service organizations for many years without fear of sanctions. If this method of sharing pertains to the CAI software in your district, you will be amazed at the richness of microcomputer instructional resources that are available if you will only look, inquire, and request what you want to use in your teaching. A list of articles that discuss the subject of software piracy and copyright protection can be found in the Recommended Readings and Media section.

WHAT CAN YOU BEGIN DOING?

If you teach a second grade class such as the example in Chapter four, you face the choice of beginning to use a microcomputer in any of the seven to ten subjects you are responsible for teaching. These are the reading, arithmetic, language arts (English), art and music, spelling and handwriting, social studies, and science courses that make up your weekly teaching plan. The only exception to courseware being available for the subjects in the list above is handwriting. There is microcomputer software available for every other subject. It is likely that you will not find programs in all these teaching subjects for your school's brand of microcomputer. Now comes the moment of choice. You will not be wise to try to use the microcomputer in every subject area at the beginning. Start with a single subject such as social studies. Obtain the use of the microcomputer for one day every three weeks and plan to use one or another of the excellent simulations that are available. Most students will view the class period spent using a social studies simulation as the high point in their week. Unless you have several machines, you will need to divide your class into teams because only part of the class can work at the microcomputer at one time. Once you have this experience well in hand, try using a reading software program during the time scheduled for reading. Again, you will need to divide the class into groups, but students are used to this in most reading classes. You may wonder, "Why not introduce the microcomputer with an arithmetic program?" You certainly could, but why do the expected thing? Perhaps you can add to the dimensions of your students' understanding of the information world around them by starting to use microcomputers in something other than an arithmetic mode.

What do you do or where do you start if your teaching

assignment is more departmentalized, like the fifth grade example in Chapter four? In that illustration, one teacher taught all the fifth grade English, another taught all the fifth grade social studies, a third taught the fifth grade science classes, and the fourth taught all of the fifth grade composition, handwriting, and spelling. Every fifth grade teacher in that school taught reading and mathematics lessons. Again, you have to make a choice. Why not start by using a microcomputer to teach a reading class session once every other week? As you gain confidence in what you are doing and as the students become more familiar with the microcomputer, there is time enough to branch out and find the courseware programs that fit your style in teaching, regardless of which special subject is your responsibility. As in the second grade description, "Why not leave using the microcomputer for mathematics until you have a solid start in another subject?" Note that, by proceeding in this way, you have all of the advantages of a unit integration approach to the use of the microcomputer in your teaching, while infusing the microcomputer into your teaching over a reasonable period of time.

There are communities, even parts of states, where the resources that can be acquired for use with a microcomputer are limited. This will not be the case for long. Every day of every month sees new educational programs announced by vendors, new microcomputers installed in schools, and new interest on the part of parents, teachers, and administrators in creating a computer-literate learning climate. Your challenge as a teacher in creating a curriculum design that will integrate microcomputers into your students' learning experiences has one further dimension. You need to look carefully and ask yourself critically if everything you have been including in your lesson plans is really that valid, useful, and relevant to the learning you want to occur in your classroom. Is some of what you have been teaching the consequence of lack of change over the years? Are some of the ways you have been teaching the result of habit? You will find that integrating a microcomputer into your instructional pattern challenges the old ways of teaching you are used to following and some of the old subject matter as well.

NOTES

1. Dr. Jerman's program, *Reading Level Analysis*, is published by Bertamax, Inc., Seattle, WA 98109. Also available from Random House School Division, Westminster, MD 21157 as *Readability Analysis Program*.
2. Combs A. What the future demands of education. *Phi Delta Kappan*. January, 1981, pp. 369-371.
3. Judd D H. Partners in Education: Instructional Uses of the Microcomputer. Chicago: Follett Publishing Company, 1981, pp. 26-27.
4. Rice J, O'Connor S. Computer literacy in the elementary classroom. AEDS-81 Convention Proceedings. Washington: Association for Educational Data Systems, 1981, p. 230.
5. *Ibid.*
6. See: Bitter G G. The road to computer literacy. *Electronic Learning*. September, 1982, p. 60; October, 1982, p. 34; November/December, 1982, p. 44; January, 1983, p. 40; February, 1983, p. 54.
7. Cupertino Union School District. K-8 computer literacy curriculum, revised 1982. *The Computing Teacher*, March, 1983, pp. 7-10.

APPENDIX

GLOSSARY*

Authoring language A language such as PILOT that is easier to use than programming languages like BASIC.

Authoring system A method of introducing text into microcomputer memory that results in a formatted screen image of a computer assisted instructional lesson (examples: CAIware, BLOCKS, Genis).

BASIC An acronym for Beginners All-Purpose Symbolic Instructional Code. A high-level, conversational programming language that is in wide use. It was created by Kemeny and Kurtz and first used at Dartmouth College in 1963.

Branch Computers follow commands given in computer program lines in numerical order. However, a "branch" command causes the microcomputer, minicomputer, or mainframe to follow instructions as directed, even though these may not be in numerical order.

Bug Any error in the program commands or syntax that is unacceptable to the logic required by a microcomputer, minicomputer, or mainframe.

Byte The basic unit of information in a computer. It commonly consists of a sequence of eight binary "bits."

Cartridge Usually a ROM chip sealed in a plastic housing that plugs into the microcomputer. It contains a permanently stored program.

Cassette A device for transferring internally stored information to and from the microcomputer's memory. This method of storage is slower than disks.

Characters Any letter, number, or graphic symbol the computer recognizes.

Chip The brain of the microcomputer; a piece of silicon smaller than one's fingernail on which thousands of electronic elements are etched.

Code lines The lines of words, symbols, and numbers that represent commands to the logic circuits of the microcomputer, minicomputer, or mainframe.

Command An instruction given to a computer through an input device or peripheral. It is executed as soon as it is received.

Computer An electronic device that receives and follows instructions to manipulate information. The difference between a computer and a programmable calculator is that the computer can manipulate text and numbers, while the calculator can only manipulate numbers.

---

*Many of these terms are commonly used but have special microcomputer meanings.

Computer-Assisted Instruction (CAI) Use of the computer or microcomputer as a medium of instruction to facilitate a dialogue similar to a student–teacher dialogue (may also be referred to as Computer-Aided Instruction).

Computer literacy Use of the computer to increase a student's familiarity with the fundamentals of information handling and with how the computer is used in our society.

Computer Managed Instruction (CMI) An instructional application that uses a computer system to store objectives, instructional materials inventory, and evaluation criteria. The computer system prepares a series of recommended instructional activities for an individual student or group of students.

Courseware A combination of content, instructional design, and the software that causes the computer or microcomputer to implement the instructions of the computer program.

Cursor A marker, sometimes square or rectangular in shape, that indicates the location on the microcomputer video screen where the system is waiting for input.

Database The collection of alphabetic and numeric data in an orderly "file drawer" format that is loaded into the memory of the microcomputer, minicomputer, or mainframe.

DATA lines The specific lines of code where information is stored, rather than commands given for microcomputer response.

Debug Correcting errors in a computer program so that the program will run properly.

Disk A record-like, magnetic, coated piece of material that can store programs, data, or tables of information.

Disk drive A device that rotates a disk so that the magnetic information stored on the disk can be read and transmitted to the microcomputer, or so that information from microcomputer random access memory (RAM) can be written to the disk.

Display Usually refers to the video screen on which characters or graphics represent output from the microcomputer, minicomputer, or mainframe.

Documentation Printed information that is provided along with the program to facilitate its use.

DOS Disk Operating System. Machine-coded programs that provide control of microcomputer use of the disk drive.

Drill A rapid student response as in a "flash card" sense is typical. Questions and answers tend to be brief in contrast to practice microcomputer programs. (See also *Practice*.)

Glossary **135**

Edit To change a program and its commands. To change the text in word processing.

Execute The act of following the instructions in the computer.

Format Preparing a magnetic track on a disk so that information can be recorded upon it (see Initialize).

Frame A term used to refer to a single screen image in planning CAI. Often found in descriptions of authoring systems and in describing the content of storyboards.

Graphics A display using lines and shapes other than the usual keyboard letters, numbers, and symbols.

Hardcopy Data or information printed on paper.

Hardware The mechanical, electrical, magnetic, and electronic devices that make up a microcomputer, minicomputer, or mainframe (includes peripherals).

IEP Individualized Education Plan. A requirement in education of handicapped children, but not limited to that use. Involves diagnosis, short-term objectives, specific educational strategy to be employed, and plan for evaluation of outcomes.

Initialize Preparing a magnetic track on a disk so that information can be recorded upon it (see also *Format*).

Input Instructions or data entered into the computer or microcomputer through a keyboard, cassette, cartridge, or disk.

K This letter was borrowed from the scientist's use of the letter to represent 1,000. Actually the letter K is used to refer to 1,024 bytes; in the binary system of counting this is the quantity of two^{10}. Now we use the letter K to refer to kilobytes of memory in a microcomputer.

Keyboard The device for typing information into a computer or microcomputer.

Line number Every line in a BASIC computer program is numbered so that the computer can follow the instructions in numerical order.

Load Process of transferring information into the memory of the microcomputer, usually from a disk, cassette, or cartridge.

LOGO A language created at the Massachusetts Institute of Technology (MIT) that permits the manipulation of a shape referred to as a Turtle (a small triangle) on the video screen. A model of a turtle can also be manipulated on the floor by the microcomputer using the LOGO language.

Loop A series of program instructions that result in repeated episodes of the same activity.

Mainframe Jargon for the large, general-purpose computer that contains the central processing unit (CPU) and the control elements of a computer system (see *Microcomputer*).

Memory The integrated circuits of a computer or microcomputer that store information.

Menu A list of choices displayed on the screen from which the user can select which program is used next.

Microcomputer A complete computer with all the components of a large mainframe computer, merely reduced in size by modern technology.

Minicomputer Smaller than a mainframe, but larger than a microcomputer.

Modem The peripheral that makes telephone connections possible between microcomputers, minicomputers, and mainframes.

Monitor A cathode ray tube (CRT) device or video screen that can be used in place of a television receiver.

Output Information produced by a computer program that is displayed on a video screen or printed on a printer. The product of data processing.

Pascal A language that provides for the structured arrangement of code lines the microcomputer, minicomputer, or mainframe can accept and act upon.

Peripheral Any device external to the microcomputer that accepts information from or sends information to the microcomputer (i.e., printer, disk drive, modem).

PILOT A language created by Dr. John Starkweather of the University of California Medical facility at San Francisco in the early 1960s. The letters stand for Programmed Inquiry Learning or Teaching.

Practice Required answers of a more complex nature than found in Drill microcomputer program exercises. The completion of multiple steps for a solution may be necessary. (See also *Drill*.)

Printer A peripheral device that prints, in typewriter-style format, the output of a computer.

Problem solving A type of microcomputer program that requires sequential entry of steps for a solution.

Program A series of instructions to a microcomputer, minicomputer, or mainframe that causes it to solve a problem or perform a task.

Programming language Set of words and symbols along with an associated grammatical structure that can be understood by the computer (e.g., BASIC, Pascal, FORTRAN, COBOL).

RAM An acronym for Random Access Memory. Information in this memory can be changed.

ROM An acronym for Read Only Memory. Information in this memory is permanently stored.

Run Jargon for "execute" a program. If this command (RUN) is followed with the name of a program, that program both loads and runs.

Save A command that results in the recording of the magnetic impulses that make up a program. The information can be stored on a cassette or a disk.

Simulation A model of random events generated by the microcomputer are introduced by depicting the impact of alternative events on a social or scientific system. The logic of the experimental method may be modeled in a laboratory simulation otherwise not feasible (e.g., effects of a nuclear accident).

Software The programs, language processors, routines, and procedures that augment a computer system or microcomputer system and allow it to be operative.

Terminal A device that permits the input to and output from a computer or microcomputer. The terminal does not need to be in the same location as the computer or microcomputer.

Time sharing A technique by which several users share the capabilities of a central computer facility. A microcomputer can serve in a time-sharing function as the central facility or as the terminal for one of several users.

Tutorial Similar to programmed instructional texts in that paragraph material with questions are under the control of a branching set of rules responsive to answers given.

Video screen The monitor or other viewing device that presents an image. Usually a cathode ray tube (CRT) that resembles a television screen.

Word-processing programs A system whereby the microcomputer, minicomputer, or mainframe computer can accept characters that form text that is useful in itself, not as computer commands, and reproduce them on the screen or printer.

RECOMMENDED READINGS AND MEDIA

BOOKS

Becker H J. *Microcomputer in the Classroom—Dreams and Realities*. Eugene, OR: International Council for Computers in Education, 1982.

Bradbeer R, DeBono P, Laurie P. *The Beginner's Guide to Computers*. Reading, MA: Addison-Wesley, 1982.

Burke R L. *CAI Sourcebook*, Englewood Cliffs, NJ: Prentice-Hall, 1982.

Buxton M. *TLC Projects for Growing Minds*. Charleston, IL: Creative Learning Association, 1983.

Carlson E H. *Kids and the Apple*. Chatsworth, CA: DataMost, 1982.

Computer Literacy Activities for Elementary & Middle School Students. Eugene, OR: International Council for Computers in Education, 1983.

Deken J. *The Electronic Cottage*. New York: Bantam Books, 1981.

Doerr C. *Microcomputers and the 3 R's*. Rochelle Park, NJ: Hayden Book Company, 1979.

Dwyer T, Critchfield M. *BASIC and the Personal Computer*. Reading, MA: Addison-Wesley, 1978.

Engel C W. *Stimulating Simulations*. Rochelle Park, NJ: Hayden, 1977.

Galanter E. *Kids and Computers*. New York: GD/Perigee, 1982.

Graham N. *The Mind Tool*, 3rd ed. St. Paul, MN: West Publishing, 1983.

Gueulette D G, ed. *Microcomputer for Adult Learning*. Chicago: Follett, 1982.

Harper D O, Stewart J H, eds. *RUN: Computer Education*. Monterey, CA: Brooks/Cole, 1982.

Heller R S, Martin C D. *Bits 'n Bytes About Computing: A Computer Literacy Primer*. Rockville, MD: Computer Science Press, 1982.

Horn R V. *Computer Programming for Kids and Other Beginners*. Austin, TX: Sterling Swift, 1982.

Hunter B. *My Students Use Computers: A Comprehensive Guide for the K-8 Curriculum*. Reston, VA: Reston, 1983.

Larsen S. *Computers for Kids*.* Morristown, NJ: Creative Computing Press, 1981.

Lathrop A, Goodson B. *Courseware in the Classroom*. Reading, MA: Addison-Wesley, 1983.

Lien D A. *The BASIC Handbook*, 2nd ed. San Diego: Computsoft Publishing, 1981.

Luehrmann A, Peckham H. *Computer Literacy*. New York: McGraw-Hill, 1983.

McWilliams P. *The Personal Computer Book*. Los Angeles: Prelude Press, 1982.

McWilliams P A. *The Word Processing Book*. Los Angeles: Prelude Press, 1982.

Mason G, Blanchard J, Daniel D. *Computer Applications in Reading*, 2nd ed. Newark, DE: International Reading Association, 1983.

Metzger M, Ouellette D, Thurmann J. *Learning Disabled Students and Computers: A Teacher's Guide Book*. Eugene, OR: International Council for Computers in Education, 1983.

MicroSift: *Evaluator's Guide for Microcomputer-Based Instructional Packages* (Revised 2/83). Eugene, OR: International Council for Computers in Education, 1983.

Moursund D. *Introduction to Computers in Education for Elementary and Middle School Teachers*. Eugene, OR: International Council for Computers in Education, 1982.

Moursund D. *Parent's Guide to Computers in Education*. Eugene, OR: International Council for Computers in Education, 1982.

Moursund D. *PreCollege Computer Literacy: A Personal Computing Approach*. Eugene, OR: International Council for Computers in Education, 1983.

Moursund D. *School Administrator's Introduction to Instructional Use of Computers*. Eugene, OR: International Council for Computers in Education, 1982.

Moursund D. *Teacher's Guide to Computers in the Elementary School*. Eugene, OR: International Council for Computers in Education, 1982.

Nave G, Browning P, Carter J. *Computer Technology for the Handicapped in Special Education and Rehabilitation: A Resource Guide*. Eugene, OR: International Council for Computers in Education, 1982.

Nevison J M. *The Little Book of BASIC Style*. Reading, MA: Addison-Wesley, 1978.

Noonan L. *Basic BASIC-English Dictionary*. Beaverton, OR: Dilithium Press, 1982.

Papert S. *MINDSTORMS: Children, Computers, and Powerful Ideas*. New York: Basic Books, 1980.

PROBE: *BASIC Programming Activities for the Microcomputer*, Glenview, IL: Scott, Foresman and Company, 1984.

Richman E. *Spotlight on Computer Literacy*. New York: Random House, 1982.

Rogers J B. *An Introduction to Computing: Content for a High School Course*. Eugene, OR: International Council for Computers in Education, 1982.

Willis J, Danley W Jr. *Nailing Jelly to a Tree*. Beaverton, OR: Dilithium Press, 1981.

Willis J, Miller M. *Computers for Everybody*. Beaverton, OR: Dilithium Press, 1983.

ELECTRONIC MEDIA

Adventures of the Mind. Springfield, VA: Children's Television International.

Braun L. *Introduction to the Computer and Its Use in Teaching and Learning, New Technology in Education—Videotape Series*. Washington, DC: US Department of Education, 1983.

Braun L. *Computer Simulations in Social Science, Science, and Math, New*

---

*Editions for TRS-80, Apple, Commodore, etc.

Technology in Education—Videotape Series. Washington, DC: US Department of Education, 1983.
Classroom Uses for Microcomputers. Chicago: Society for Visual Education, 1982.
The Computer and You. Freeport, NY: Educational Activities.
Computer Literacy—Introduction to the Computer. Princeton, NJ: Innovative Programming Associates, 1982.
Computers: From Pebbles to Programs. New York: Guidance Associates.
Daiute C. *Using the Computer to Develop Writing Abilities, New Technology in Education—Videotape Series*. Washington, DC: US Department of Education, 1983.
Don't Bother Me, I'm Learning. Del Mar, CA: McGraw-Hill Films.
Gould L. *Research and Development: Interactive Computer Graphics for Institutional Problem-Solving, New Technology in Education—Videotape Series*. Washington, DC: US Department of Education, 1983.
Hakansson J. *Computer Gaming as an Integrated Learning Experience, New Technology in Education—Videotape Series*. Washington, DC: US Department of Education, 1983.
Holznagel D. *The Computer as a Tutor, New Technology in Education Videotape Series*. Washington, DC: US Department of Education, 1983.
The Information Machine. New Hyde Park, NY: Modern Talking Pictures.
Lowd B, Sturdivant P, Bowen B. *School District Experiences in Implementing Technology, New Technology in Education—Videotape Series*. Washington, DC: US Department of Education, 1983.
Luehrmann A. *Computer Literacy: A New Subject in the Curriculum, New Technology in Education—Videotape Series*. Washington, DC: US Department of Education, 1983.
Man and Computer, A Perspective. New Hyde Park, NY: Modern Talking Pictures.
Some Call If Software. New Hyde Park, NY: Modern Talking Pictures.
Watt D. *LOGO: The Computer as an Intellectual Tool, New Technology in Education—Videotape Series*. Washington, DC: US Department of Education, 1983.

RECOMMENDED READINGS—CHAPTER ONE

A day at the Pulaski St. Learning Center. *Electronic Learning*, February, 1982, p. 36.
Gawronski J D, West C E. Computer literacy. *ASCD Curriculum Update*, October, 1982, pp. 1-8.
Judd D H, Walker J E. Use of the microcomputer to enhance the language experience approach to teaching reading. *Ohio Reading Teacher*, 11-13, October, 1982, pp. 11-13.
Kohl H. The computer as palette and model builder. *Learning*, March, 1983, pp. 46-50.
Luehrmann A. Computer literacy. *The Computing Teacher*, March, 1982, pp. 24-26.

Melmed A S. Information technology for U.S. schools. *Phi Delta Kappan*, January, 1982, pp. 308-311.
Miller B S. Bringing the microcomputer into the junior high: A success story from Florida. *Phi Delta Kappan*, January, 1982, p. 320.
National Science Foundation. The Process of Technological Innovation: Reviewing the Literature. Washington, DC: National Science Foundation, 1983.
Office of Technology Assessment. Informational technology and its impact on American education. *The Computing Teacher*, January, 1983, pp. 18-29.
Pritchard W H Jr. Instructional computing in 2001: A scenario. *Phi Delta Kappan,* January, 1982, pp. 322-325.
Shane H G. The silicon age and education. *Phi Delta Kappan,* January 1982, pp. 303-307.
Sommerfeld L L. To byte or not to byte. *Educational Horizons*, Spring, 1983, pp. 116-117.
Taylor R P, ed. *The Computer in the School: Tutor, Tool, Tutee.* New York: Teachers College Press, 1981.
Walla K, Brubaker V. Toward a computer literate society—an elementary school responsibility. *The Computing Teacher*, December, 1982, pp. 57-59.
Winkle L W, Mathews W M. Computer equity comes of age. *Phi Delta Kappan*, January, 1982, pp. 314-315.
Zucker A A. The computer in the school: A case study. *Phi Delta Kappan*, January, 1982, pp. 317-319.

RECOMMENDED READINGS—CHAPTER TWO

Allard K, Reid R. Courseware evaluation: The SECTOR project. *Educational Computer Magazine.* March/April, 1983, pp. 22-26.
Douglas S, Neights G. *A Guide to Instructional Microcomputer Software.* Harrisburg, PA: PA Department of Education, 1982.
Fisher G. "Lemonade For Sale" and other simulations. *Electronic Learning.* February, 1983, pp. 78-82.
Heck, W P, Johnson J, Kansky R J. *Guidelines for Evaluating Computerized Instructional Materials.* Reston, VA: National Council of Teachers of Mathematics, 1981.
Kleiman G, Humphrey M M, Buskirk T. Evaluating educational software. *Creative Computing.* October, 1981, pp. 84-90.
Lough T. Exploring new horizons with LOGO. *Electronic Learning.* April, 1983, pp. 70-75.
Lough T. LOGO, discovery learning with the classroom's latest pet. *Electronic Learning.* March, 1983, pp. 49-53.
Swett S. LOGO offspring: A look at modified versions of LOGO and "Turtle Graphics" programs. *Electronic Learning.* May/June, 1983, pp. 72-75.
Theme Issue on LOGO. *Classroom Computer News.* April, 1983.
Theme Issue on LOGO. *The Computing Teacher.* November, 1982.
Theme Issue on Software. *Electronic Learning.* October, 1982, pp. 39-59.

Todd N. Hello LOGO. *Educational Computer Magazine.* March/April, 1983, pp. 40-41.

Watt D. LOGO: What makes it exciting? *Popular Computing.* August, 1983, pp. 106-113, 148-166.

Watt M. Making a case for software evaluation. *The Computing Teacher.* May, 1982, pp. 20-22.

RECOMMENDED READINGS—CHAPTER THREE
Pilot

Camuse R A. An Apple PILOT Primer. *Educational Computer Magazine.* September/October, 1982, pp. 20-23; November/December, 1982, pp. 16-18; January/February, 1983, pp. 28-29.

Hawkins R. PILOT—the language of computer aided instruction. *80 Microcomputing*, July, 1981, pp. 122-136.

Keyser E. Microcomputers and PILOT. *AEDS Monitor.* Jan/Feb/Mar, 1979, pp. 22-23.

Poole A. Turtle PILOT. *Compute.* September, 1982, pp. 64-87.

Smith M. PILOT Tutorial I. *Creative Computing.* November, 1982, pp. 181-182.

Smith M. PILOT Tutorial. *Creative Computing.* December, 1982, pp. 243-251.

Wilkinson P. Everyone's language: PILOT. *Creative Computing.* May, 1979, pp. 93-95.

Authoring Systems

Gagne R M, Wager W, Rojas A. Planning and authoring computer-assisted instruction lessons. *Educational Technology.* September, 1981, pp. 17-26.

Hartman K. Authoring considerations in writing instructional computer programs. *The Computing Teacher.* September, 1982, pp. 27-29.

Herriott J. CAI: A philosophy of education—and a system to match. *Creative Computing.* April, 1982, pp. 80-86.

Issacson D. *How to Design Educational Microcomputer Programs.* Fresno: California State University, 1982.

Judd D H. Teacher created programs: Suggestions for success! *Educational Computer Magazine.* Nov/Dec, 1982, pp. 34-35, 44.

Judd D H. Learning to program really isn't necessary or BASIC isn't basic anymore. *Educational Computer Magazine.* September/October, 1981, pp. 10-11.

Kleiman G, Humphrey M. Writing your own software—authoring tools make it easy. *Electronic Learning.* May/June, 1982, pp. 37-41.

Savage E R. Education 80. *80 Microcomputing.* February, 1982, p. 354.

Schleicher G. Authoring systems can save time in development of CAI. *Electronic Education.* November, 1982, pp. 20, 27.

Word Processing

Boudrot T E. The magical typewriter. *Electronic Learning.* February, 1983, pp. 84-87.

Bradley V. Improving students writing with microcomputers. *Language Arts.* October, 1982, pp. 732-43.

Daiute C. Word processing: Can it make even good writers better? *Electronic Learning.* March/April, 1982, pp. 29-31.

Judd D H. Word processing in the classroom: Is it really practical? *Educational Computer Magazine.* May/June, 1982, pp. 18-19.

Mander C. An Oakville enterprise: Computers teach pre-schoolers to read and write. *Canadian Library Journal.* February, 1982, pp. 17-18.

Mason G E, Blanchard J S. Reading teachers put the computer to work. *Classroom Computer News.* May/June, 1982, pp. 44-45.

Monahan B D. Computing and revising. *English Journal.* November, 1982, pp. 93-94.

Prentice L R. Poet, a program for word people. *Classroom Computer News.* September/October, 1981, pp. 18-20.

Shostak R. Computer assisted composition instruction. In: Computers in *Composition Instruction.* Lawlor J, ed. Los Almitos, CA: SWRL Educational Research and Development, 1982, pp. 5-18.

Shostak R. "Tough old birds" may succumb to computer's charm. *Electronic Education.* March 1982, pp. 27-28.

Wall S M, Taylor N E. Using interactive computer programs in teaching higher conceptual skills: An approach to instruction in writing. *Educational Technology.* February, 1982, pp. 13-17.

Watt D. Word processors and writing. *Popular Computing.* June, 1982, pp. 124-126.

Wise D. "Special new WP package makes kids want to write. *InfoWorld.* November 22, 1982, p. 13.

Woodruff E, Bereiter C, Scardamalia M. On the road to computer assisted compositions. *Journal of Educational Technology Systems.* Winter, 1981, pp. 133-148.

Word processing: the A to Z of software. *Personal Computing.* March, 1982, pp. 72-104.

Zacchei D. The adventures and exploits of the dynamic storymaker and textman. *Classroom Computer News.* May/June, 1982, pp. 28-30, 70.

RECOMMENDED READINGS—CHAPTER FOUR

Bracey G W. Computers in education—what the research shows. *Electronic Learning.* November/December, 1982, pp. 51-54.

Coogan B. Getting started with microcomputers. *Electronic Learning.* March, 1983, pp. 30-35.

Kearsley G, Hunter B, Seidel R J. Two decades of computer based instruction projects: What have we learned? *THE Journal.* January, 1983, pp. 90-94; February, 1983, pp. 88-96.

Kulik J A, Kulik C C, Cohen P A. Effectiveness of computer-based college teaching: A meta-analysis of findings. *Review of Educational Research.* Winter, 1980, pp. 525-44.

Oliver P. An administrator's round table—technology and education. *Electronic Learning.* February, 1983, pp. 63-67.

Radio Shack. *K-8 Math Cross-Reference.* Ft. Worth: Tandy Corporation, 1981.

Silverman S, Dunn S. Raising SAT scores. *Electronic Learning.* April, 1983, pp. 51-55.

Teacher's Friend, Richardson, TX: The Soft Spot, 1983†

Theme Issue on The Year in Review. *Electronic Learning.* May/June, 1983, pp. 43-61.

Theme Issue on Computers and Special Needs. *The Computing Teacher.* February, 1983.

Willis J, Johnson L, Dixon P. Computer managed instruction: Can you use it? *Educational Computer Magazine.* May/June, 1983, pp. 13-16.

RECOMMENDED READINGS—CHAPTER FIVE

Gangel D M. Administrative use of micros 'lopsided'. *Electronic Education.* May/June, 1983, pp. 32-33.

Immel A R. Is software piracy justified? *Popular Computing.* July, 1983, pp. 48-54.

Lanza L G. Elementary school computer literacy: A case study of success. *Educational Computer Magazine.* Mar/Apr, 1983, pp. 14-15.

Sturdevant R. Microcomputers and copyright in education. *Phi Delta Kappan.* January, 1982, p. 316.

Wright E B, Forcier R C. Teacher-education curriculum for the 80's. *Educational Computer Magazine.* Jan/Feb, 1983, pp. 56-58.

MATERIALS RESOURCE LIST

Authoring Systems

Author I, Radio Shack Division, Tandy Corporation, 1 Tandy Center, Fort Worth, TX, 76102.

BLOCKS Authoring System, California School for the Deaf, 39350 Galludet Drive, Fremont, CA, 91538.

CAlware-2D, Fireside Computing, Inc., 5843 Montgomery Road, Elkridge, MD, 21227.

Courseware Development System (Genis), Bell & Howell Company, 7100 N. McCormick Road, Chicago, IL, 60645.

---

*Provides excellent example of scope and sequence chart applied to K-8 arithmetic texts

†Provides excellent example of scope and sequence chart applied to English as a second language

Recommended Readings and Media   145

Bibliographic Sources

Michael Arsulich, "Microcomputers in Education"; a 20-page offprint available from Instructional Resource Center, Department of Education, San Diego County, San Diego, CA, 92101.

ERIC, Educational Resources Center, National Institute of Education, Washington, DC, 20208; consult also ERIC Clearinghouse on Information Resources, Syracuse University, School of Education, Syracuse, NY, 13210; and ERIC Clearinghouse on Elementary and Early Childhood Education, University of Illinois, College of Education, Urbana, IL, 61801.

Microcomputer Index, Santa Clara, CA. A quarterly index also available on Dialog Information Services, Inc., a subscription information retrieval service headquartered in Palo Alto, CA.

Elizabeth S. Wall, *Children's Books for Computer Awareness and Literacy*. A free copy has been available. Write to Bayshore Books, P.O. Box 848, Nokomis, FL, 33555.

Magazines and Periodicals

ACM SIGCUE Bulletin, Association for Computing Machinery, P.O. Box 12015, Church Street Station, New York, NY, 10249.

AEDS Journal, 1201 Sixteenth Street, NW, Washington, DC, 20036.

AEDS Monitor, 1201 Sixteenth Street, NW, Washington, DC, 20036.

Byte Magazine, 70 Main Street, Peterborough, NH, 03458.

Classroom Computer Learning, 19 Davis Drive, Belmont, CA, 94002

Commander, P.O. Box 98827, Tacoma, WA, 98498.

Compute, P.O. Box 5406, Greensboro, NC, 27403.

Computers, Reading, and Language Arts, P.O. Box 13039, Oakland, CA, 94661.

Creative Computing, P.O. Box 789-M, Morristown, NJ, 07960.

Digest of Software Reviews: Education, 1341 Bulldog Lane, Suite C, Fresno, CA, 93710.

Educational Computer Magazine, 3199 DeLaCruz Boulevard, Santa Clara, CA, 95050.

Educational Technology, 140 Sylvan Avenue, Englewood Cliffs, NJ, 07632.

80 Micro, 80 Pine Street, Peterborough, NH, 03458.

80 US Journal, 3838 South Warner Street, Tacoma, WA, 98409.

Electronic Education, 1311 Executive Center Drive, Tallahassee, FL, 32301.

Electronic Learning, 902 Sylvan Avenue, Englewood Cliffs, NJ, 07632.

The Family Programmer (formerly TI Source and LOGO News), 33 Maple Avenue, Armonk, NY, 10504.

InCider, 80 Pine Street, Peterborough, NH, 03458.

InfoWorld, 375 Cochituate, Framingham, MA, 01701.

Journal/20, Box 1149, Van Alstyne, TX, 75095.

Journal of Computer-Based Instruction, Western Washington University, Bellingham, WA, 98225.

Micro, P.O. Box 6502, Amherst, NH, 03031.

Microcomputing, 80 Pine Street, Peterborough, NH, 03458.

The Midnite/Paper, 1280 Richland, Ave., Lincoln, IL, 62656.

Appendix

99'er Magazine, P.O. Box 5537, Eugene, OR, 97405.
PC, One Park Avenue, New York, NY, 10016.
PC World, 555 DeHaro Street, San Francisco, CA, 94107.
Personal Computing, 50 Essex Street, Rochelle Park, NJ, 07662.
Popular Computing, 70 Main Street, Peterborough, NH, 03458.
School Courseware Journal, 1341 Bulldog Lane, Suite C, Fresno, CA, 93710.
Softalk, 11021 11160 McCormick Street, North Hollywood, CA, 91603.
SQ Syntax Quarterly, RD2, Box 457, Harvard, MA, 01451.
Teaching and Computers, 730 Broadway, New York, NY, 10003.
T.H.E. Journal, P.O. Box 992, Acton, MA, 01720.
The Computing Teacher, Department of Computer and Information Science, University of Oregon, Eugene, OR, 97403.
TRS-80 Microcomputer News, One Tandy Center, Ft. Worth, TX, 76102.

Organizations

Association for Computers in Mathematics and Science Teaching, P.O. Box 4, Austin, TX, 78765.
Association for Educational Communications and Technology (AECT), 1126 Sixteenth St. NW, Washington, DC, 20036.
Association for Educational Data Systems (AEDS), 1201 Sixteenth St. NW, Washington, DC, 20036.
Association for the Development of Computer-based Instructional Systems (ADCIS), Western Washington University, Bellingham, WA, 98225.
CONDUIT, P.O. Box 388, Iowa City, IA, 52244.
EPIE and Consumers Union, P.O. Box 839, Water Mill, NY, 11976.
MicroSift, Northwest Regional Educational Research Laboratory, 300 S.W. Sixth Avenue, Portland, OR, 97204.
Minnesota Educational Computing Consortium (MECC), 2520 Broadway Drive, St. Paul, MN, 55113.
National Association for Educational Computing, 33 Knutsen Street, Tappan, NY, 10983.
National Council of Teachers of Mathematics, 1906 Association Drive, Reston, VA, 22091.
SOFTSWAP Microcomputer Center, San Mateo County Office of Education, 333 Main Street, Redwood City, CA, 94063.
Almost every national and many regional or state associations involved with education have set up special interest groups concerned with the use of microcomputers in education.

Word Processing

Apple Writer, Apple Computer Inc., 10260 Bandley Drive, Cupertino, CA, 95014.
Atari Word Processor, Atari Computer, Box 427, Sunnyvale, CA, 94086.
Bank Street Writer, Scholastic Inc., 730 Broadway, New York, NY, 10003 (also Broderbund, 1938 Fourth Street, San Rafael, CA, 94901).
EasyWriter, IBM, P.O. Box 1328, Boca Raton, FL, 33432.

EasyWriter II, Information Unlimited Software, 2401 Marinship Way, Sausalito, CA, 94965.
Electric Pencil, IJG, Inc., 1260 West Foothill Blvd., Upland, CA, 91786.
Letter Perfect, LJK Enterprises, P.O. Box 10827, St. Louis, MO, 63129.
Magic Window, Artsci, Inc., 5547 Satsuma, North Hollywood, CA, 91601.
Paper-Mate, AB Computers, 252 Bethlehem Pike, Colmar, PA, 18915.
Scripsit and *SuperScripsit*, Radio Shack Division of Tandy Corporation, 1800 Tandy Center, Fort Worth, TX, 76113.
TI Writer, Texas Instruments, 2301 North University, Lubbock, TX, 74908.
Wordpro, Commodore Business Machines, 681 Moore Road, King of Prussia, PA, 19406.
Wordstar, MicroPro, 33 San Pablo Road, San Rafael, CA, 94903.

MICROCOMPUTER MANAGEMENT PROGRAMS FOR PRINT LEARNING RESOURCES

Teachers and curriculum directors will want to search for microcomputer management programs that monitor and report on student progress in using arithmetic, reading, and other textbook series. Examples include the following:

"*Course Manager.*" Scott, Foresman and Company, Electronic Publishing Division. Provides management of Books 3-8 of the Scott, Foresman Mathematics series.

"*Reading—Microcomputer Management System.*" Scott, Foresman and Company, Electronic Publishing Division. Provides tracking, monitoring, and evaluation of student progress at every book level of *Scott, Foresman Reading*.

INDEX

activities
   for microcomputer familiarization by students, 19-29
   for programming by students, 82-91
   for program use or modification by teachers, 110-114
   for software use by students, 52-58
administrator, CAI benefits for, 106-109
Alpha-Synturi keyboard, student use of, 14
"Animals," 23-24
Apple computers
   children's writing program for, 75
   directory of programs of, 45
   sample program of, 106
AppleDOS3.3 Disk Master, activity for, 23-24, 29
Apple "LISA," 108
Apple Silentype Printer, student use of, 13
Apple II, student use of, 13, 14
Apple II+, student use of, 16-18
arithmetic. *See also* mathematics
   activities using microcomputer for, 27-28, 53-54
   in second grade, microcomputer for, 98-99
Atari, writing program for use on, 75
Atkinson, R.C., 94, 95
authoring systems, 62
   for CAI programs, 65-72
   PILOT as, 63-65

"Bank Street Writer," 13, 74-75
   example of, 76-77

Barnes, O.D., 94
BASIC
   versus authoring systems, 66, 72
   graphics and, 50
   to improvise CAI program, 24
   programming in, simple, 53
   student use of, 34
   teacher-made programs in, 61-62
      converting between PILOT and, 90-91
      problem-solving using, 85-86
      word problem using, 88-89
   ways to use, 42-43, *44*
BASIC programming statements, 62
bilingual students, microcomputer programs for, 107
Bitter, Gary, 127, 128

CAI, 93-114. *See also* instruction
   activities for, 24, 110-114
      converting storyboard to program, 111-112
      creating worksheet or quiz, 113
      evaluating software programs, 112-113
      improvising, 24
      modifying CAI program, 110-111
      using "Quizstat." 113-114
   activity for running, 55
   for drill and practice, 56-57
   for simulation, 57-58
   administrator benefits of, 106-109
   authoring systems for, 65-72
   color and, 51
   control of students by, 34, 40
   definition of, 96

in elementary school studies, 94-95
in high school studies, 95-96
in junior high school studies, 95
student benefits of, 104-105
summary on, 109
teacher uses of, 2, 4-8, 96-104
CAI checksheet, 68-71
career selection programs, 105
checksheet, CAI, 68-71
CHROMAtrs unit, 51
"Civil War," 5
CMI (computer managed instruction), 81, 98, 101, 104
COBSE (Council for Basic Skill Education), 34
college entrance tests, 105
color, as software consideration, 50-51
Color-Graf unit, 51
Combs, Arthur, 126
Commodore, programs of, 45
Computer Practice Keyboard Company, 78
CONDUIT organization, 4, 40
Control Data Corporation, 40, 67
Copying, 48-49
Copyright law, 48-49
corrections, with word processor, 74, 75-77, 79
"COURSEWRITER," 67
CP/M microcomputer, "Grammatik" for, 79
Crawford, A.N., 95
creativity, in writing, 77-78
Cupertino Union School District, 128
curriculum design and development, by teachers, 126-130
customizing of program, 48-49

Dale-Chall "easy word list," 122, 123
database programs, 117
definition of, 117
DATA lines, customizing by means of, 49
dictionary, electronic, 79, 80
"Distance and Direction," 16
drill and practice
CAI benefits in, 96-97
CAI program for, running, 56-57
courseware for, 34-36
in elementary school studies, using CAI, 94-95
in junior high school studies, using CAI, 95
microcomputer use for, 8-9

"Dueling Digits," 56

economic education
example of student use of microcomputer for, 16-17
programs for, 5, 106
editor, prose, 79-80
Educational Computer Magazine, 47
Educational Testing Service, on Pascal, 42
Electronic Learning, 127
elementary school, studies of CAI in, 94-95
for fifth grade, 100-104, 131
for second grade, 98-100, 130
English drill-and-practice program, in elementary school study, 94
enriched study materials, 105, 106
ESCAPE keystroke, double, 74

fifth grade, microcomputer use in, 100-104, 131
"Fish," 5
Fitzgibbon, N.H., 94
Flesch readability formula, 122
Fletcher, J.D., 94, 95
Fog index, 122
Franklin Ace microcomputer, 51
"Furs," 5

gifted students, 105, 106
global search, in word processing, 126
"Gradebook," 117-120
"Grammatik," 79-80
graphics, as software selection consideration, 49

handicapped students, microcomputer programs for, 107-108
Harris, R.Y., 94
Hatfield, L.L., 95
high school studies of CAI, 95-96
Hum/RRO (Human Resources Research Organization), 127

IBM-PC microcomputer
for educational administrators, 108
"Grammatik" available for, 79
individualized education plans (IEPs), microcomputer uses in, 103

150 Index

infusion, definition of, 127
instruction by microcomputer,
    1-29. *See also* CAI
  creating a teaching and learning
    climate for, examples of,
    11-29
  curriculum design and development for, 126-130
  gradebook program for, 118-120
  location and scheduling factors
    in, 10-11
  readability evaluation and,
    120-126
  society and, 2-4
  subject areas, grade levels, and
    student types and, 4-8
  teacher-made programs for,
    61-91
    activities for, 82-91
    authoring systems for, 65-72
    PILOT as authoring aid in,
      63-65
    summary on, 81-82
    word-processing programs for
      student reading and writing,
      72-78
    word-processing programs for
      teacher-generated print
      materials, 78-81
  types of programs, 8-10

Jerman, Max, 121-123
junior high school studies of CAI,
    95

"Kaboom," 18
Kemeny, J., 42
keyboard
  activities for learning, 20-21
  Alpha-Synturi, example of
    student use of, 14
  children's use of, 78
Kurtz, T., 42

Language Experience approach
    to teaching reading, 14
learning climate creating, 11-19
learning reinforcement, CAI in,
    104
Learning Resource Center,
    example of microcomputer
    use in, 18
"Lemonade Stand," 16-17, 39, 106
letter writing, printer for quality,
    81
"LISA," 108

Litman, G.H., 95
LOGO
  activity using, 52
  for learning keyboard, 21
  student use of, 34
  ways to use, 40-43, *40*

mathematics. *See also* arithmetic;
    economic education
  in elementary school study,
    using CAI, 94
  example of microcomputer use
    for, 12-13
  in high school study, using CAI,
    96
  in junior high school study,
    using CAI, 95
  Radio Shack program for, 15
Mathematics, National Council of
    Teachers of, on software
    evaluation, 48
MECC (Minnesota Educational
    Computer Consortium)
  "Selling Lemonade" of, 106
  as source of microcomputer
    programs, 5
  simulation courseware from, 39
Microsift evaluation format, 47, 48
"Minerals," 5
"Moptown," 55
Morningstar, M., 94
"MusicMaster," 14

NCTM (National Council of
    Teachers of Mathematics),
    on software evaluation, 48
"Nomad," 5
Northwest Regional Educational
    Laboratory, 47

"Odell Lake," 5, 39
"Oregon," 5, 39

Pachter, S.N., 96
Pascal, 42, 43
PET, by Commodore, student use
    of, 16
Phi Delta Kappan, 126
PILOT
  versus authoring systems, 66, 69, 72
  graphics and, 50
  student use of, 13, 34
  teacher-made programs in,
    61-66, 82-91
    converting between BASIC
      and, 90-91

examples of simple and additional programming, 82-85
problem-solving using, 85-86
word problem using, 87-88
ways to use, 42-43
PILOT core statements, 62, 63
PILOT J command, activity using, 89-90
"Planit," 67
PLATO series, 4, 67
print materials, word-processing programs for teacher-generated, 78-81
problem solving
  activity for, 54
  CAI benefits in, 98
  courseware for, 36-37
  microcomputer for, 9
  in programming solution, activity for, 85-86
program(s). *See also* software
  converting storyboard to, 111-112
  "locked," 48-49
  modifying CAI, 110-111
programming
  in PILOT
    additional, 83
    simple, 82-83
    of word problems, 87-89
    problem solving in, activity for, 85-86
    of word problems, using PILOT and BASIC, 87-89
prose editor, 79-80
publishers
  on microcomputers, 129
  as source for software, 45-46
  of traditional educational materials, software available through, 5-7, *6*

quiz, creating, 113
"Quizstat," 113-114
quiz writing programs, 126

Radio Shack
  catalog by, 45
  mathematics program of, 15
  MC10 of, and color, 51
Radio Shack Color Computer, 51
readability analysis programs, 120-126
reading
  in elementary school study, using CAI, 94-95
  microcomputer uses for, 6-7

examples of, 11-14, 18
in second grade, 98-99
word-processing programs for, 72-78, 82
"Reading is Fun," 11-12
reading level of textbooks, microcomputer used in evaluation of, 120-126
record keeping
  in authoring systems, 81
  CMI for, 98
  microcomputer for, 117-118
research, on CAI, 93-96

Scholastic Aptitude Test (S.A.T.), 105
School Courseware Journal, 56
science
  in high school study, using CAI, 95
  programs for, 5, 57
  simulations for, 9-10
Science Research Associates Achievement Series test, 95
"Scripsit" program, 74, 75
  example of, 76
seat assignment functions, 119
second grade, microcomputer use in, 98-100, 130
"Sell Apples," 5
"Sell Bicycles," 5
"Selling Lemonade," 106
"Sell Plants," 5
simulation, 9-10
  CAI program for
    benefits of, 97-98
    running, 57-58
  courseware for, 38-40, *39*
Skinner, B.F., 36
SMOG grade, 122
social studies programs, 5, 16, 57
society and microcomputers, 3-4
  activity on, 19-20
software, 33-58. *See also* instruction
  activities for, 52-58, 112-113
  available types of, 4-10, *6*
  customizing, 48-49
  for drills, 34-36
  evaluating, 47, 112-113
  LOGO, PILOT, and BASIC, 40-43, *40, 44*
  for problem-solving, 36-37
  selection criteria for, 46-48
  for simulation, 38-40, *39*
  sound, color, and graphics factors in, 49-51
  sources of, 44-46, 129

Index

software (*continued*)
  summary, 51-52
  for tutorials, 37-38
sound, as software selection consideration, 50
Spache formula, 122
special education, 103. *See also* handicapped student
spelling
  electronic dictionary for, 79
  example of student use of microcomputer for, 17
"Spell-N-Time," 17, 56-57, 110
"Sprite" mode of LOGO, 41
Starkweather, John, 63
storyboard, 68
  converting to programs, 111-112
  making, 68, *69*
student. *See also* activities
  bilingual, 107
  CAI benefits for, 104-105
  creating learning climate for, 11-19
  evaluation of, by microcomputer, 103
  handicapped, 107-108
  studies, on CAI, 93-96
Summerlin, L.R., 95
Suppes, P., 94
syllabication, 123

teacher
  activities for use by, 19-29. *See also* activities
  curriculum design and development by, 126-130
  instructional programs made by, 61-91. *See also* instruction, teacher-made programs for
  microcomputer uses for, 1-2, 4-8, 96-104
    examples of, 11-19
    for record-keeping and nonteaching duties, 117-131
    reports by, on microcomputer use, 102-104
"Teacher's Aid," 117
teaching/learning climate, creating, examples of, 11-29, *12*
tests. *See also* quiz
  analysis of questions on, 125
Texas Instruments, catalog by, 45
textbooks, reading level of, microcomputer use in evaluation of, 120-126

TI-99/4A microcomputer, 11
"Ticcit," 67
"TIP" program, 67
"Trail West," 16
TRS-80
  activity for TRSDOS disk of, 29
  "Grammatik," available for, 79
  program for, for teaching writing, 75
TRS-80, Model I, 12-13
  color and, 51
  example of student use of, 12-13
TRS-80, Model III
  color and, 51
  example of student use of, 15, 17, 18
"Turtle Graphics" mode of LOGO, 41
"Tutor," 67
tutorial(s), 8-9
  CAI as, 97
  courseware for, 37-38
  in high school study using CAI, 95-96
typing. *See also* keyboard
  microcomputer keyboard and, 78
  in study using CAI, 95

unit integration, definition of, 127

"Vocabulary Skills," 55
"Voyageur," 5

Wheeler-Smith formula, 122
Wilkinson, J.H., 95
Wilson, H.A., 94
Wolcott, J.M., 95
word problem, programming of
  using BASIC, 88-89
  using PILOT, 87-88
word processing
  activities in, 84-91
  global search capability in, 126
  readability approach to, 124
  for student reading and writing, 72-78, 82
  for teacher-generated print materials, 78-81
  teacher use of, 62
worksheet, creating, 113
writing
  letter quality, printer for, 81
  by students, word-processing programs for, 72-78, 82